Composing Music for Worship

Composing Music for Worship

Editors:

Stephen Darlington and Alan Kreider

CANTERBURY
PRESS
Norwich

© the Contributors 2003

First published in 2003 by the Canterbury Press Norwich
(a publishing imprint of Hymns Ancient & Modern Limited,
a registered charity)
St Mary's Works, St Mary's Plain,
Norwich, Norfolk, NR3 3BH

www.scm-canterburypress.co.uk

British Library Cataloguing in Publication data

A catalogue record for this book is available
from the British Library

ISBN 1-85311-524-X

Typeset by Regent Typesetting, London
Printed and bound in Great Britain by Biddles Ltd
www.biddles.co.uk

For Professor Paul S. Fiddes

Christian student of culture,
visionary, encourager and enabler,

in warm gratitude

Contents

About the Contributors   ix

Foreword   xi

1 Introduction   1
Alan Kreider

2 Music and Mystery   15
Howard Goodall

3 God, Theology and Music   35
James MacMillan

4 Darkness to Light, Cycles and Circles:
The Sacred in My Music   51
Robert Saxton

5 Requiem for Magnificat   66
Andrew Carter

6 Beyond a Mass for Westminster   76
Roxanna Panufnik

7 Worship in Spirit and in Truth   86
Graham Kendrick

8 The Lost Tradition of Lament   104
John Bell

CONTENTS

9 The Future of the Hymn   117
   Janet Wootton

10 Is there a Future for the Church Musician?   141
   John Ferguson

11 Renewing the Past in the Present:
   The Living Art of Church Music   155
   John Harper

   Notes   173

About the Contributors

John L. Bell, Glasgow: composer of hymns and songs; member of The Iona Community; convenor of editorial committee, *Common Ground*; theologian and teacher of music in congregations

Andrew Carter, York: composer of *Missa Sancti Pauli*, *Benedicite* and many anthems and carols

Stephen Darlington, Oxford: Organist and Tutor in Music, Christ Church; University Lecturer in Music; director of music, Christ Church Cathedral; recording artist

John Ferguson, Northfield, Minnesota: Elliot and Klara Stockdal-Johnson Professor of Organ and Church Music, St Olaf College; composer of anthems; designer and presenter of hymn festivals

Howard Goodall, London: composer whose works include *Missa Aedis Christi* and *The Lord is My Shepherd* (The Vicar of Dibley); TV presenter

John Harper, Dorking: Director General, Royal School of Church Music; Professor of Music, University of Wales, Bangor; composer of works for liturgical use

Graham Kendrick, Croydon: composer of hymns and songs; worship leader

Alan Kreider, Elkhart, Indiana: former director, Centre for the Study of Christianity and Culture, Regent's Park College, Oxford; now Adjunct Faculty in Church History, Associated Mennonite Biblical Seminary

James MacMillan, Glasgow: composer of many works, including *Veni, Veni Emmanuel*, *Raising Sparks*, *Seven Last Words from the Cross*; composer-in-residence, BBC Philharmonic Orchestra

Roxanna Panufnik, London: composer whose works include *Westminster Mass* and *The Music Programme*

Robert Saxton, Oxford: composer of many works, including *The Circles of Light*, *Concerto for Orchestra*, *Music to Celebrate the Resurrection of Christ*; University Lecturer in Music; Fellow of Worcester College

Janet H. Wootton, London: minister of Union Chapel, Islington; editor of *Worship Live*; theologian and hymn writer

Foreword

Religious faith is experience before it is theory, or even theology, and at the heart of this experience is the encounter between the self and the other; both the transcendent other, God, and our fellow believers. Frequently this encounter is mediated through worship, and while both word and action are vital, and though silence can be profound, it is often music which unites both word and action, self and the other, in ways which touch us at the very depths; music can allow the silence to be even more meaningful and resonant.

It was therefore most appropriate that the first aspect of faith and culture to be explored in the opening days of the new millennium in the Centre for Christianity and Culture at Regent's Park College, Oxford, was that of 'Composing Music for Christian Worship'. It was even more significant that the theme was explored not only at a theoretical or even theological level, but also at the experiential level. This happened in the lectures themselves in various ways, through recorded music and live performance, as well as audience participation; but perhaps most memorable were the shared experiences of choral evensong at Christ Church Cathedral in which the discussions came to life in fresh ways in a living act of worship.

Now these wide-ranging and thought-provoking insights into music and worship are made available to a wider audience through this book, which includes not only the contributions made during the eight weeks of Hilary Term 2000, but further material in additional chapters which helpfully supplement and extend the discussion. The Centre for Christianity and Culture at Regent's Park College exists to explore the complex relationship between faith and its cultural settings in a multi-disciplinary way, and this book bears witness to the continuing importance of that task. Whether addressing its social context through literature or philosophy, science or the arts, the place of faith in the modern and post-modern world in which we live remains a vital issue, and this book takes its place amongst other publications, public lectures and regular conferences, as part of the ongoing life and research of the Centre.

Alan Kreider, my predecessor as Director of the Centre, and Stephen Darlington, Director of Music at Christ Church, are to be congratulated in the vision which gave birth to the original lectures and services in Oxford, and coupled with that our thanks to them and to the Canterbury Press for bringing these lively and stimulating reflections to a durable form in the shape of this book which deserves to be read widely and deeply.

Nicholas J. Wood, Director
Centre for Christianity and Culture
Regent's Park College, Oxford
Hilary Term 2003

I

Introduction

ALAN KREIDER

For those of us who love music and are Christian, the third Christian millennium is a fascinating time. Never in humanity's history has music been as omnipresent. As we walk down the street, the sound of boom boxes surrounds us; as we board a plane or sit in the dentist's chair, we will hear Brubeck or Mozart or soft rock. Whether we like it or not, music often seems unavoidable. But at the same time, organized religion is increasingly avoidable, at least in Western Europe. Decade by decade attendance at Christian worship services continues to fall; a recent authoritative survey of church attendance in England is significantly entitled *The Tide Is Running Out*.[1] Even in the United States, where church parking lots are often still full, recent surveys indicate that there are fewer worshippers than there were several decades ago.[2]

In the new millennium, with music more widely available than ever and with Christian churches increasingly less frequented, what is the role of those who compose music for Christian worship? This was the question in the back of our minds as people gathered, week by week in the early months of 2000, at Regent's Park College in Oxford to listen to the composers whose lectures comprise this book. The first lecturer, eighteen days into the new millennium, was Howard Goodall, composer of the theme song for 'Red Dwarf' as well as a Mass for Christ Church. He was succeeded by eminent representatives of various approaches of writing music for the

Church – from the modern classical composer Robert Saxton to the singer-songwriter Graham Kendrick. (At a later date, the widely performed and influential Scots composer James MacMillan and the eminent American church musician John Ferguson added essays to the collection.) After each lecture, many of us hurried down Cornmarket and St Aldate's to Christ Church, where the Cathedral Choir, directed by Stephen Darlington who planned the series with me, performed music by the day's composer in Evensong. For those of us who took part in the series it was an unforgettable experience. And I believe that the ensemble of its lectures makes for an intriguing book that helps us understand the musical and religious life of our fascinating era.

In this introduction I will attempt to give a foretaste of what will emerge in the papers. In doing so I will quote the lecturers and draw from their insights. But I will also discuss some ongoing questions raised in the lectures – questions that will require additional thought as we compose and perform music in Christian worship.

Postmodernity and Post-Christendom

These are widely recognized characteristics of life at the turn of the third Christian millennium.[3] Many lecturers alluded to the first of these, *postmodernity*. Some, such as Howard Goodall, welcomed its possibilities; others gave less attention to its effects. But the influence of postmodern culture, it seems to me, is pervasive in these essays, as well as in the musical worship of churches in Britain and North America today. Postmodern culture rejects the unchallengeable givenness of dominant cultures and narratives; it is open, flexible and eclectic; it is pragmatic and therefore subjective and experiential; it is mesmerized by technique and technology, especially electronic technology. A spirituality of feeling is à la mode; a spirituality of 'truth' is less fashionable.

These postmodern characteristics affect the life of the churches in many ways, including their musical worship. The suspicion of dominant cultures has led to a widespread willingness to query institutions and traditions; just because Lutherans have sung chorales since the sixteenth-century Protestant Reformation there is no reason why they should continue to do so today. Instead there is restlessness and questioning: How does the music 'work'? What are its effects? How does it make me feel? What if I don't like it?

Further, the availability of electronic media has given us unprecedented control over our musical environment. We all – listeners as well as composers – now have access to the widest possible range of music, across the centuries as well as across cultures and geography. What a musical cornucopia is now available to us! We can keep these musics in separate categories – hymns in church, techno-rock in the dancehall, and Bollywood film tracks in the Indian restaurant. Or we can bring them together. Just as the French master Olivier Messiaen incorporated Hindu rhythms and birdsong in his music for the Roman Catholic Church in France, we too have the possibility of convergence in music in other settings, including church.

We can also be perfectionists. We can listen to the finest of musical executants performing whatever we wish whenever we wish. Why should I laboriously practise the piano when I can listen to Evgeny Kissin? There is therefore now almost certainly less piano playing, less guitar strumming and less singing than there was only a generation ago. And if we do not like what we hear, we (at least in our private environments) can simply turn it off or switch stations. The pain of this, Robert Saxton reports, was clear to Benjamin Britten, who bewailed a civilization in which one could turn off Bach's *St Matthew Passion* in mid-narrative. Postmodern people live in a consumer culture; we are demanding, and we want value for money. We are probably less tolerant of music that we dislike than our parents were; and we, surrounded by so much music which we acquire so cheaply, may savour music less deeply than they did.

Fewer lecturers explicitly referred to the second dominant characteristic of our times – *post-Christendom* – but its effects underlay them all. Until quite recently in Western Europe and North America one could speak without hesitation of the local culture as Christian. Even though many people neither believed nor went to church, the dominant 'noise' of the civilization was a Christian noise.[4] Laws favoured Christian practice, for example, ensuring that stores would be closed on Sunday; Christian ministers graced public occasions; authors filled their writings with Christian allusions, which they were confident that most readers would comprehend. In the United Kingdom there were additional refinements to Christendom: the Christian religion had to be taught in school, where children had to learn Christian hymns and take part in assemblies; bishops of the Established Church voiced Christian perspectives in debates in the House of Lords. On both sides of the Atlantic, the Christianity of Christendom was buttressed by a kind of matter-of-fact obviousness under-girded by a more or less subtle inducement and compulsion.[5]

These traits of Christendom are now rapidly disappearing. Globalization and immigration have made both Britain and the United States into multicultural and multifaith societies. I was reminded of this recently in Manchester, in England's industrial North, when the hairdresser cutting my hair lectured me on the superiority of Islam to Christianity and invited me to his mosque. And in America, it is not only immigrants who embrace Buddhism or Islam. At the same time, aspects of society that once favoured Christians, whether the prohib-ition of Sunday trading or the use of Christian language in the public domain, are withering. It is not surprising that attend-ance at Christian worship has fallen, decade by decade. *The Tide Is Running Out*, a profile of Christian worship on a typical Sunday in September 1998, revealed that 7.5 per cent of the English populace attended one service that day. This was down from 12 per cent two decades earlier; and, in view of the age profile of those who were there (a preponderance of people over sixty, a paucity of children and youths) the number of Sunday worshippers is likely to fall still further.[6] Of course, the number of Sunday worshippers in absolute terms is still large; and this number rises to approximately 16 per cent of the populace when those who worship regularly on a monthly or annual basis are taken into account.[7] The trajectories, however, are downwards – in church and Sunday school attendance, infant baptisms, and confirmations. In America, religious observance, although more widespread than in most parts of Europe, is less buoyant than it seemed to be two decades ago. The effects of these changes are increasingly evident in people who are in church: they are there, not because habit or a headmistress requires it, but because they have chosen to worship God instead of washing their cars. Post-Christendom is an era of religious voluntarism.

Postmodernity, post-Christendom – it is a fascinating time to be a Christian in Western cultures. In our time, three aspects of this fascination are increasingly evident. One of these, to which Janet Wootton points us in her lecture, is the globalization of Christianity. Europe may, as the *Church Times* recently put it, 'lead the world in godlessness',[8] but throughout much of the world Christian expressions of godliness are growing numerically. In Asia and Africa Christian numbers are increasing, rapidly in some places; and today the centre of gravity of the Christian Church runs through the southern hemisphere. Christians in the West are now turning to their global partners for insight in church life and evangelism; they also are discovering in the South new possibilities for their songs and worship. As never before, Christianity is a global, rather than a Western, phenomenon.[9]

A second fascinating aspect of the current scene, represented in these essays by Graham Kendrick, is loosely called Pente-costalism. This (together with its charismatic counterparts in the historic denominations) has had roots and analogues throughout much of Christian history, but in its current form it burst out of a revival in southern California in the first decade of the twentieth century. It is this kind of Christianity that is behind much of the global growth of the Church, and that characterizes areas of Christianity that continue to flour-ish in the West. It is marked by an emphasis upon the tangible reality of God, who acts in people's lives; by worship that places a deeper value upon the emotional than the cognitive dimensions of life; and by what Harvey Cox has called 'the remarkable centrality of *music*, not just as embellishment but as the wavelength on which the message is carried'.[10]

A third aspect, less significant than the former two but nonetheless fascinating, is the emergence, in the post-Christendom West, of classical music with explicitly Christian themes. As Roxanna Panufnik has observed in her interview, Westerners who do not go to church buy CDs of Gregorian chant, Hildegard of Bingen and John Tavener – and buy them in astonishing quantities. Tavener, indeed, figures in a number of the essays in this volume. His work, shaped by his espousal of the faith and thought-world of Greek Orthodoxy, has come to be exclusively Christian in its references. And his music draws crowds and sells recordings. Also popular is the music of other 'holy minimalists', notably Arvo Pärt and Henryk Górecki. At the same time, classical music in the argumentative traditions of Western music and of explicitly Christian content has emerged in the countries of the former Soviet Union, where Sofia Gubaidulina and Alfred Schnittke were prophetic voices. Something similar is happening in post-Christendom Scotland, where James MacMillan testifies that when he spoke in a TV interview of being guided by 'divine inspiration' to write music which passionately engages with the Passion of Christ his interviewer adjudged him to be 'avant-garde'! Artists are often at the forefront of social reflection and comment. In post-Christendom, where observant Christians are in a minority, a number of composers have emerged as prophets who speak to a baffled but ready audience.

Like postmodernity, post-Christendom has had its effects upon the composing of music for Christian worship. One of these, about which John Harper speaks from his privileged perspective as Director General of the Royal School of Church Music, is that in many churches throughout England the 'standard provision' of musical resources (choir, organ, hymn book) has simply disappeared. Declining attendance, and the tendency of people who attend church to listen to music rather than perform it, has led to a dearth of musicians to lead the congregations by their playing and singing. Congregations cope with this situation by various means, some of which (characteristically of our era) are electronic. Some rely upon electronic sound generators that can conjure accompaniments for an entire songbook; others sing along with CDs of the monks of Taizé or the music group of Holy Trinity Brompton. But many people are not content with these electronic solutions. As a result, the music that is written for practical use in many churches in the future will have to be designed for small groups of at times inexpert performers.

A second effect is the fragmentation of styles and understandings of worship. Not so long ago, through the influence of school assemblies and Sunday school, the majority of Welsh and English children knew the same hymns, which they then sang in church or on the terraces of football stadiums. No longer. As Janet Wootton has noted, in multicultural Britain the hymn's future, though vital, will be in specialized sectors of the Christian Church – while other sectors of the Church will abandon the hymn entirely for forms of charismatic song. This fragmentation is also evident in the Church of England. For its new *Common Worship* John Harper reports that he and others were asked to devise settings of sung Eucharistic prayer using many styles – 'rhythmic and upbeat', modern French, worship song, 'Taizé-like', Orthodox or worship song, in addition to the traditional Sarum chant. Individual congregations in various traditions have worship patterns that reflect the global Church. The different forms of music required by these styles are a reflection of differing understandings of worship. Some place a premium on the intellect, while others are convinced that worship is in essence emotional; some cherish liturgy, while others are mystified by it.

Third, the *voluntarism* of the post-Christendom era places special demands on the composer of music for worship. The congregation is no longer a captive audience. If its members do not like what happens in church, they will move their custom elsewhere – or experience God while hiking in the hills! More than ever, as Roxanna Panufnik reports from her parish, it matters what the people like, and what they want to hear and sing. Of course, there will be many 'taste cultures' in differing Christian churches. In some places, such as the 'centres of excellence' of the cathedral and collegiate foundations of the Church of England, choral evensong will be sung 'properly', and new music will continue to be written for these services. Some people in post-Christendom will continue to gravitate to the old choral foundations because they are drawn to Purcell and Herbert Howells. But in most churches, because of shifts in Christian demography, musical worship of this sort will be impossible. And, indeed, many Christians will prefer to worship using other kinds of music.

So at the beginning of the twenty-first century, Western societies on both sides of the Atlantic are vastly different from what they were, say, at the end of the Second World War. There are places, some of them churches, where it seems that little has changed. There are rich, deeply layered traditions in the music of the churches. People respond differently to them. Take the biblical canticles, for example. The Quaker Andrew Carter has come to find the endless repetitions of the

Magnificat to be tedious, and Janet Wootton has written a hymn calling for a 'Moratorium on the Magnificat', to be sung until there is evidence that the mighty are being put down and the hungry are being filled with good things; James MacMillan, on the other hand, who is deeply committed to social justice, finds inspiration in this annunciation text. One could find similarly divergent responses to hymns and psalms. What is the cultural relevance of tradition? In our context of postmodernity and post-Christendom, what is the way forward for composers of music for Christian worship? What music will speak deeply to people who are faithful members of their churches and will build these churches into embodiments of Christian culture? What music, by the same token, will intrigue new people by the Christian good news and attract them to the churches?

Inculturation

A useful way to think about the task facing composers for worship today is *inculturation*. The Christian churches have always interacted with culture. In doing so they have had to make choices. When Augustine of Canterbury came to pagan England in 596 as the papally appointed missionary of Catholic Christianity he had to decide what to do with the temples that he found. Should he destroy the temples, if the authorities permitted this? Or should he, as Pope Gregory the Great suggested, adopt another approach – not destroy the temples, but destroy the idols within them? According to the latter approach, Augustine would accept the pagan buildings, but cleanse them by sprinkling holy water and depositing relics, 'since, if these temples are well built, it is needful that they should be transferred from the worship of idols to the service of the true God'.[11] Was this an example of Pope Gregory's wisdom? Or should Augustine, for the sake of the integrity of the gospel, have broken more decisively with aspects of Anglo-Saxon culture than he did? Missiologists and historians continue to debate this, for the issue that Augustine and Gregory were facing is perennial.

This much is clear. Across the centuries and continents, churches in their mission in society have at times attempted to impose upon people ideas, rituals and norms which they find alien. Most people today find this to be objectionable, an example of 'cultural imperialism'. On the other hand, churches have often flowed too smoothly with the values of their societies, surrendering commitments and practices that are central to the Christian faith. This can be equally objectionable, an example of 'syncretism' or at worst 'Christo-paganism'.[12] Christians, missiologist Andrew Walls has argued, must seek to find their way between these extremes, guided by two principles: the *indigenizing* principle, which affirms that the gospel can be at home in any culture; and the *pilgrim* principle, which asserts that there will be tension between the Christian gospel and every culture.[13] Christianity thus must express itself in any culture in ways that are comprehensible to that culture, and in ways that are shaped by that culture; at the same time Christianity must maintain the winsome but surprising angularities of Jesus Christ and his gospel and the traditions and practices that sustain these. How, in our setting, does this kind of thinking affect the music that composers write for our churches?

As we survey our churches today, a number of approaches are evident. One approach *segregates*. Such segregation can happen temporally: at 8 a.m. a Church of England parish will have Holy Communion according to the *Book of Common Prayer*, which reflects the cultural conditioning of a previous era; at 8 p.m. it will have a youth service, in which the influence of contemporary musical culture is thunderously evident. This approach divides the congregation into age groups and 'taste cultures'. Another form of segregation in which age and taste are evident is the long-established division according to congregational approaches or denominational tendencies: some churches revel in the hymn, and their members are not allergic to holding hymn books; other churches do not want to sing hymns or indeed anything else written before 1995, and their members want their hands to be unencumbered as they sing. Some churches are at home with liturgy, with its roots in Christian traditions that are venerable and cosmopolitan; while others repudiate self-conscious liturgy as irrelevant infringements upon the Holy Spirit's (and their) freedom. Such segregation allows disparate traditions to develop in parallel; and each of them, as they face questions of continuity and change, have the opportunity to be 'living traditions' (Saxton). These separate church cultures can be beautiful and valid, from which other people, if they are humble and attentive, can learn.

A second approach *integrates*, in various forms of *coexistence* and *convergence*. This approach seeks not to jettison traditions but to bring them into creative dialogue with new impulses coming from contemporary culture. Sometimes this happens by artful juxtaposition, as a congregation learns to intersperse renewal songs with Wesley hymns. Such juxtaposition often requires good diplomacy between power blocs – the organist and the music group, for example, may be predisposed to be at loggerheads with each other; it requires Christians, without wincing or walking out, to sing things they would prefer not to sing; it often requires truthful speech and love, as members of different generations and cultures listen to each other's stories about what they value in a particular song or approach to worship. At times coexistence will become convergence, as when an old hymn tune will be retrieved by reharmonizing it and giving it a Celtic flavour, which, Graham Kendrick says, 'reflects people's search for roots and certainties, and for deeper theological content'. Of our lecturers, Howard Goodall has stated a vision that entails both coexistence and convergence; Graham Kendrick has called for convergence; and church music statesman John Harper has advocated flexibility, adaptation, and borrowing from other traditions as 'something that is distinctive in style and idiom' emerges.

Discernment

But whatever approach we adopt, discernment is necessary. For, as the theologians remind us, no culture – whether that of the traditional churches or that of contemporary society – is above the judgement of the gospel. By that standard, some aspects of culture, Jesuit thinker John Francis Kavenaugh has commented, are 'human', others are 'inhuman'. Some are 'graced', others are 'disgraced'.[14]

Such discernment is vital as we reflect on our churches' cultures and the music that we use – whether we are consciously influenced by contemporary secular culture or not. What in our musical worship enriches our humanity and infuses it with God's grace? Is our musical life life-giving? Is it musically and textually worthy? Is it appropriate and in good taste? Is it comprehensible to regular worshippers and to outsiders? Is it offensive (on sexist or racist lines)? Does it seem elitist ('the rich man in his castle') or, in its warrior language, militaristic? Is it in harmony with the God of the Bible and the teaching and way of Jesus Christ? Does it give voice to the full range of human experiences and emotions, to lament as well as to celebration? Does it build community, and enable people of all ages to participate and to contribute their gifts? Does it reflect Andrew Carter's concern that we all see through the eyes of children? Does it give expression to the struggle of the Christian Way, and wrestle with Christ's Passion as well as celebrating his resurrection and exaltation? Does it enable people to meet God, who is present in our weakness and who empowers the least? Does it equip people to be disciples of Jesus Christ in their homes and relationships and work? Does it enable them, in their life amidst contemporary cultures, to discern what they can embrace as 'graced' and what they must learn to resist as 'disgraced'?[15]

Perhaps above all, does the music that composers write for our churches equip a community to be faithful to God across the generations? In the essays in this book, there are celebrations of the old – Monteverdi's *Vespers* (Goodall) or the hymns of Isaac Watts (Wootton) or plainsong (MacMillan). These can be enjoyed for their own sake; they can also be worked with by composers today – as James MacMillan quotes, dissects and builds with Gregorian chant. However we approach the old, we want to be wise stewards of the past, the best products of which we will bequeath to our children

that the next generation might know them,
    the children yet unborn,
and rise up and tell them to their children,
    so that they should set their hope in God.
                    (Psalm 78.6–7, NRSV).

God's Creator Spirit was at work in the past as well as the present, and we would be impoverished by its loss.

But the old must be complemented by new creation, by new works that God's Spirit inspires in us today. These new works will be in new idioms, musical and cultural, and will reflect a changing culture and society. This process requires a constant learning and broadening as well as a conserving of that which is good. The Church will be like the experts in the Jewish law who were also trained for the kingdom of heaven; they, said Jesus, were 'like the master of a household who brings out of his treasure what is new and what is old' (Matthew 13.52).

Inevitably, much music that is composed will fall by the wayside. Janet Wootton reminds us of the eight thousand hymns that Fanny Crosby wrote, of which only one or two have been incorporated into the living tradition. And it is evident that not every carol that is written for each year's Service of Lessons and Carols at King's College, Cambridge enters the active repertoire. Nevertheless, as churches whose members seek to worship God and to live and share the gospel test the old and evaluate the new, a certain 'classicizing' will take place as they develop their life-giving *core*. As John Bell commented in his lecture, 'Like good poetry, [good music] can be explored time and again and delivers something of freshness with each performance, and accrues all the while layers of association and fondness.' What comprises this body of classics will vary from congregation to congregation and denomination to denomination.

Differing Christian cultures will continue. Some will be large and 'successful'. Others will be domestic and experimental. Those that most effectively survive will not necessarily be those that have the music which is most beautiful, or that is most like the music which most people hear most of the time. For ultimately it is not music that attracts people to church. In a postmodern, post-Christendom electronic age people can get music anywhere. People are rather attracted by an amalgam of many realities – people's hunger for God; their need of whole relationships; their concern for integrity and truth in the midst of anomie and confusion; their sense that Christianity, in the face of other options, makes sense and somehow 'works'. Such Christian communities will be sustained by practices that become habitual, and enable them to pass the faith from one generation to the next; they will also be perennially renewed by new artistic creativity in tune with missional practice. Within such communities music will be composed which is strong. As Christians perform this music and worship with it, it will enable their varied communities to flourish and believers to live their faith. And sometimes, in ways that are surprising and unpredictable, this music – composed for Christian worship – also will enrich the lives of masses of aesthetically and spiritually sensitive people who never will attend services in Christian churches.

2

Music and Mystery

HOWARD GOODALL

I have spent the last 14 months making a TV documentary series and writing an accompanying book on the history of Western music – a kind of musical 'Life on Earth' entitled *Howard Goodall's Big Bangs* – a process which has temporarily interrupted my normal compositional routine, but which has also been a fascinating, if exhausting, privilege. As the long research and filming period was coming to an end, I began, perhaps inevitably, to think a little more clearly about the conclusions that could be drawn from looking at such a broad canvas of musical culture. It is far easier to look back on a thousand-year story of musical 'progress' and 'achievement' than it is, however, to assess the present moment. A distinctly Western European music, broadly speaking, was born in the Church. Though it later flew the nest and found a permanent home in the secular world, it was for the first few hundred years of its existence nurtured by the Christian Church. Does music still have a powerful role to play in Christian worship? Does Christianity still have a powerful role to play in the further development of music, or are its parenting skills largely forgotten? Does the current state of affairs, that is, a period of cross-fertilization and convergence between the Western European tradition and its counterparts in Africa, the Americas and the East, between 'classical' and 'pop' or between 'acoustic' and 'techno', have anything to offer the modern composer of sacred music?

I may indeed be a living example of the trend towards convergence, product as I am of a mixed marriage of classical training and popular taste. One moment I am writing the theme music for the comedy series 'Red Dwarf', the next I am writing a mass for the choir of Oxford's Christ Church Cathedral. One day I am commissioned to compose the jingle for a TV commercial campaign, the next I am rehearsing a piece of musical theatre at the Royal Opera House. The arrangement I came up with for the opening ceremony of the Millennium Dome was scored for 500 singers from different choirs (children's, Welsh male voice, gospel, chamber, mixed, opera chorus, boys', girls'), a symphony orchestra, two opera soloists, one soul and one pop soloist, a classical bass-baritone and the Jools Holland band, complete with blues rhythm section and horns. The song itself was the gospel classic *Amazing Grace*, intertwined with a South African children's song, *Siyahamba*, sung in English and Zulu.

Of course I write music that is influenced by my classical training, as a chorister, as a pianist and as an organist. But I am also very influenced by the fact that I've grown up during the 1960s, 1970s and 1980s and like all musicians these days I am deeply affected by popular music, which undoubtedly has been the predominant influence on twentieth-century music. I don't think of myself as being torn between these worlds, or being pressurized to adopt a particular style or attitude for 'classical' concert music and another for commercial 'popular' music. I think of all these overlapping fields as complementary and mutually beneficial. The interplay within me between different musical traditions is a wholly creative and positive one. My experience is that the rubbing of creative shoulders in the wider culture is also wholly creative and positive. The currency of my working life is music – a music without artificial frontiers. A good example of this might be the theme music for the BBC series *The Vicar of Dibley*. This is an immensely popular TV comedy, at the moment attracting upwards of ten million viewers an episode, so it is undeniably at the centre of our mainstream popular culture – and yet the music I composed for it is a straightforward, unapologetically non-comic setting of Psalm 23. It is now (I am happy to report) performed in its own right in a fuller-length version all over the world, in churches, schools and concert halls. I would no sooner write self-consciously 'comic' or 'populist' music for a popular comedy series than I would write self-consciously 'serious' or 'difficult' music for a commission to be premiered in a concert hall. I am a product of my time – all around me jazz, rock, choral, orchestral, rap, blues, ethnic musics are engaging with each other as equals. Classical music is merely taking its place in the overall picture, not leading from the front, as once it did.

Mainly as a result of Edison's invention of recorded sound at the end of the nineteenth century, all creative musicians of the twentieth century have immersed themselves in the music of other cultures and traditions, forging new styles from their experience. Two composers who demonstrate this are Olivier Messiaen (1908–92) and John Tavener (b. 1944) – both intensely religious composers, both schooled in a rigorously European classical tradition, but whose later influences radically altered the direction of their work. Messiaen, a devout Catholic of the old school whose principal influence was clearly Claude Debussy (1862–1918), like Debussy became fascinated with the musical palette of the Far East – with Indian rhythm patterns and Javanese gamelan sounds. These sources come bursting into his work (quite unexpectedly) with his *Turangalîla-Symphonie* of 1948. Tavener, on the other hand, became fixated with the music of the Greek Orthodox Church, utterly rejecting (in his ruminations on the subject) the Western classical heritage of his earlier output. In his view European music went off the rails irredeemably well before Mozart. He has equally dogmatic views about the superficial 'borrowing' of exotic musical raw material from around the world, exempting himself from the charge. It is perhaps not surprising that a composer who is enjoying enormous success and popularity with the help of sources from a foreign culture to his own, even one in which he had saturated himself, would feel uncomfortable about other people doing the same. Having said that, he is so remarkably humble in his love of and respect for Greek Orthodox culture and liturgy that he may be less tolerant towards other composers who are less humble and less indebted to their sources.

As for Messiaen, what emanates from his *Turangalîla-Symphonie* is a profound love of the world and its infinite variety. It is an exuberant shout of joy and praise to a God who created first birdsong then every note created and performed by humankind. Of course Messiaen lived in a more naïve era when communications were considerably less sophisticated than they are now. Now we can download or browse music from practically any place in the planet. For Messiaen the journey was a more effortful and challenging one, and it is often the case that projects that require effort and time and patience yield the best results. To some extent the history of Christianity is one of its connecting with other cultures, customs and philosophies and its being transformed by the relationship, so it is only appropriate that Christian music should also be developed by its interplay with non-European influences. The most obvious example of this is the impact of African music on sacred music in the last 150 years.

Ultimately, though, it isn't for Tavener or Messiaen or myself to judge to what extent we may or may not trawl through the riches of the world's cultures to enhance our work; it will be for history to decide what amalgam became the leading current of the next wave of music. Remarkably, the *Turangalîla-Symphonie*, written after Messiaen's release from internment by the Nazis in the Second World War, seems to set the agenda for the music of the following half-century. Sounds and effects from the music of Java ricochet

across its orchestral spectrum, colliding with the spooky resonances of the electronic ondes martenot and a huge battery of
assorted percussion instruments. It is multicultural music at its
most abandoned and uncompromising. That the work was
preceded by his overwhelmingly sombre *Quartet for the End of
Time* for traditional Western chamber instruments makes its
noise and craziness even more astonishing. We cannot at this
point judge if the widespread expropriating of the music of,
say, tribal Africa will have a debilitating or inspirational effect
on Christian music in the long run, we simply observe that it
is the fashion of our highly communicative times. It is a matter
of degrees. For us, India and its culture are relatively remote
and foreign; for the fifteenth-century English composer John
Dunstable (1390–1453), France was a relatively inaccessible,
alien place. When his music was exported to northern France
with the English garrison installed at the conclusion of the
Hundred Years War, it seemed weirdly different and exotic,
immediately catching the ear and transforming the style of the
premier French composer of the day, Guillaume Dufay
(1400–74).

So taking as read the notion that I consider myself a composer living and working within a vigorously mixed and open
musical environment, it feels right to examine for a moment
what lies behind the sacred choral music that runs in my blood
and to which I constantly return for nourishment and fulfilment.

What is the point of sacred music? Why not speak your
prayers and preach your gospel without it? Well, for a start,
singing is not a more sophisticated, luxury version of speech –
it is in many ways more fundamental, more instinctive to us
than spoken communication. There are peoples around the
world, like the Hopi Indians of northern Arizona and some
Aboriginal tribes, who believe the world was 'sung' into
creation. In Hindu mythology all things grow from a universal
'OM'. Babies often respond to their mother's singing long

before they are able to pick up the nuances of speech. To this day a remote tribe in China, the Dong, use singing as the primary method of communication above speech (which they consider crude and misleading). Most verbal exchanges in their village take place through singing, so much so that if you intend to marry someone in the Dong tribe, first you have to undergo a singing audition with their family elders to determine the quality of your voice and therefore your suitability for marriage. This might be the only community in the world in which choral scholars get the absolute pick of the eligible talent. Singing coaches are available, apparently, to improve the performance of auditionees before the big proposal. Since singing, then, is utterly central to the human experience, it is hardly surprising that it has become central to Christianity in all its forms. European music, the music of early Christendom, separated itself from the music of other continents about a thousand years ago when it developed a form of notation, thus beginning an extraordinary journey leading to the colossal and sophisticated masterworks of Palestrina, Bach or Mozart. But it never lost its roots in a simpler, more spontaneous form of sung worship, the kind of chant and response that characterizes the religious music of other cultures even today.

The first, most obvious reason to employ music in your sacred ritual would be as an expression of ecstasy and joy, to glorify God as triumphantly as one could. The thrilling opening of Monteverdi's 1610 *Vespers* is as good an example as any. It is triumphant and celebratory, with trumpets, drums, organ, brass and choir – it unequivocally declares 'God is great'. It is the musical equivalent of the building, St Mark's Basilica in Venice, for which it was written – something awe-inspiring, something that says that 'this faith is the most important element in our culture'. There is a sense of unqualified majesty and wonder. But it is also quite a one-dimensional way of looking at music for worship, and probably one that is nowadays to some extent marginalized. Since the Enlightenment, composers have been drawn to more complex visions of the role of music in the Church. Indeed you could say that they have always been more interested in the power of music when expressing grief, suffering and passion than when employed as mere cheerleaders at the altar. Even *Godspell*'s unabashed joyousness is beefed up by a balladic core centring on the betrayal and loneliness of Jesus of Nazareth.

Another reason you might introduce music into church worship is as a calling card or invitation to outsiders to see what's on offer – as a kind of commercial for Christianity. Look at our magnificent architecture, interior design by Renaissance masters no less, ravishing gold altarpiece and splendid comfortable oak pews. But all this is nothing compared with the seductive power of our music. Martin Luther understood the allure of music in church better than anyone. For him, music was a high priority, an evangelical tool of great effectiveness, so he famously took all the best tunes of the day (folk, popular, secular, sacred – it mattered not), gave them new Lutheran texts and absorbed them into the new Protestant church's hymn (or chorale) collection. The rich tradition of hymn singing that has underpinned centuries of Anglican worship around the world is largely an inheritance from the Lutheran mission to get congregations singing great tunes.

Music has often been employed by the Church as an agent of conversion. Even today the evangelical and Pentecostal movement is unabashed in its use of gospel music to attract potential converts. I once went into a high security prison in Croydon with a Seventh Day Adventist Gospel Choir whose express aim was to bring the inmates closer to their message through irresistibly joyful music. Whether these, society's most dysfunctional and damaged minds, are more or less open to the powerful, emotional effect of gospel music, and whether one should therefore proceed with particular caution when offering fast-track hope and salvation, is another matter. The Anglican chaplain of the prison held strong views on the subject but was nevertheless willing to embrace the mission from time to time.

Gospel songs, like a great deal of sacred music, operate on a number of levels. For the outsider, they might provide access in an enjoyable, uplifting way. For the already converted their role is to induce in the worshipper a state of mind, a willingness to listen, an openness of heart in preparation for a spoken message of urgency or importance. Because of this, musical delivery is afforded high priority in gospel churches. In evangelical, Pentecostal, charismatic or Adventist churches music is not a spectator sport. Members of the community are totally immersed and actively involved in the sound, rather as they might be in water for an adult baptism. The songs are therefore rehearsed and prepared with tremendous care and attention to detail. A musical director of a gospel church would identify much more readily with the concentrated purpose and rigour of, say, Stephen Darlington preparing the Christ Church Cathedral Choir for a service, than with the half-hearted, sloppy and under-rehearsed efforts of many an Anglican parish choir. I do not blame the organists and clergy of these harassed and overstretched parishes. They are doing their best in difficult circumstances – operating in communities who do not accord importance to sacred music; who do not volunteer to join in; or who do not care enough about high standards to put in the time and energy required to achieve them. The total lack of commitment and enthusiasm shown by the majority of Christian church congregations with respect to hymn singing across Europe is anathema to congregations in the diverse black churches in the same territory. Older West Indians now living in Britain recall with world-weary resignation the frosty reception they received when they first arrived as immigrants in the 1950s. Their disappointment, though, was turned to total bafflement when they turned up at their local parish churches to confront not just the knee-jerk unfriendliness, but dull, gloomy, funereal services with grimly passive singing and a disinterested congregation. No wonder they set up their own church communities as soon as they could.

At the simplest level, music as a tool of conversion is traditionally used – alongside storytelling – in the teaching of the very young. 'Away in a manger' is for many children an 'entrypoint' into the caring, comforting philosophy of Christianity, with its easy and gentle tune. Until relatively recently, children in Britain were brought up on a diet of hymns and sacred songs at school assembly. While it is understandable that a modern multicultural society might not feel it appropriate to start a child's day with so partisan a religious vision, there is also a great loss here too. For the first time in many thousands of years, children are not now able to sing together as a group. Communal singing is a fundamentally good thing for people to do. It is all very well for hymns to be replaced as a musical source but they have been replaced with nothing.

An odd aspect of modern culture is that we hear powerful sacred music all the time. We are still in thrall to its depth and beauty, but we are often as not completely unaware that it is sacred music. Television viewers watching a commercial using a section of Mozart's or Verdi's *Requiem* or even Lloyd Webber's *Pie Jesu* are being delighted, moved, manipulated or excited by church music and yet they will be loathe to admit it. They might admire Mozart's artistry but they almost never give due credit to the Church for its music, even on a purely cultural level. It is also true, though, that we are more likely to hear the sacred music of Tavener or Gregorian chant in a secular environment (driving along in the car listening to Classic FM, for example) than in a religious building. For whatever reason, music's power to invite in potential believers isn't working as well as it used to. The listener is quite content to soak up the soothing balm of Górecki's *Totus Tuus* without giving a second thought to its text, its meaning or its underlying purpose. But to what extent must we comprehend those elements of a piece of music to surrender to its message?

The battle between easy comprehensibility on the one hand and a sophisticated, hidden mysteriousness on the other continues all around us in the year 2000 almost as if the Reformation were still a current event. Is sacred music only effective if it is truly accessible and truly inclusive, or can it be equally powerful when appearing as if it is a complex, enigmatic code? I have discussed the issue of the use of Latin and the tension between traditional and contemporary in sacred music in my book *Howard Goodall's Big Bangs*[1] so I will not cover the same ground again here. Suffice it to say that I believe it is possible for congregationally motivated Christian rock or gospel music to coexist happily with the ancient choral tradition brilliantly exemplified by the choir of Christ Church Cathedral here in Oxford. The two approaches are not mutually exclusive in the same way that a lover of rap music does not have to destroy classical orchestral music to express that love. The broad church of music in Britain is an immensely positive thing. What I do know from my own experience, both as a musician and as someone involved in sacred music specifically is that you cannot replace the excellence of one tradition with a second-rate version of the other. Excellence and integrity in one field breeds excellence and integrity in the other. I really don't mind what style of music worshippers want to bring in to their churches as long as they do it to the highest standard they can. In France, their once-magnificent cathedral choir tradition has been entirely lost to a music of droning banality and awfulness or no music at all. Musicians in the churches, cathedrals and abbeys of France have been replaced by non-musicians. The French church has been immeasurably impoverished by this trend.

This point about inclusiveness, though, is an important one, because one role for music in church is indeed to let the congregation feel they are an integral part of the transaction:

that they are not simply being lectured to or preached at by a priest. One sad result of the kind of interminable service with little or no musical ingredient which one endures in a continental church is that the concentration and focus of the event lapses. In purely theatrical terms, the set, the costumes, the sound of the solo actor's monologue, the unfolding narrative and drama of the Mass are melted into one unchanging mood, one colour, one view. Even the most dedicated of churchgoers cannot possibly find this uplifting. It can feel like a punishment, the most numbingly tedious play one ever attended. Music can give shape, drama, colour and movement to the occasion. It can bring passages of scripture into sharp relief, or create an atmosphere of hushed expectation. More than that, if a congregation are to sing themselves, it allows them to interact with the drama and to include their feelings in the service. There is an interesting parallel here with the Jewish experience. One of the most striking aspects of worship in many synagogues is that members of the congregation feel quite free to chat among themselves despite the efforts of the rabbi to involve them in what he is reading or in prayer. It is apparently so accepted a way of going about the proceedings that members of the congregation do not even consider it particularly discourteous to mutter and gossip during the rabbi's utterances. However, on those few occasions when I have witnessed a musical component in synagogue (for example at a wedding), immediately these most musical of all people afford it their full attention. One cannot help but conclude that if God himself had an urgent message to convey to his chosen people he would be advised to turn it into a song lyric and set it to music – that way he'd have a fighting chance of being noticed. Perhaps that's what the Psalms are.

Sometime today (18 January 2000) the Archbishop of Canterbury and the Pope will have knelt together in prayer, so it is an appropriate day to add to our list of reasons for writing church music that of its unifying role. Christianity is made up of an extraordinary melting pot of different nations, communities, sects and ideologies. Christian music, on the other hand, unlike language or cultural tradition or historical imperative, is more or less completely transportable. It is the common currency of all churches, loved by all, used by all, embraced by all. Music is class and accent free. Christians from all backgrounds and denominations can be moved and inspired by the Greek Orthodox-influenced music of John Tavener; by the Russian Orthodox-influenced music of Sergei Rachmaninov; by Orlando Gibbons' delicately beautiful music of the English Protestant Settlement; by Palestrina's amazing masses, rigorously conforming to the Vatican's Counter-Reformation strictures on musical complexity; by the gospel music of a Caribbean island's corrugated-tin church; by the stirring melodies of the Welsh Methodist hymn book; by Handel's *Zadok the Priest*, written by a German émigré in Hanoverian England to shore up a distinctly monarchist vision of God; by Bach's uncompromisingly Lutheran masterpieces; by Arvo Pärt's Baltic mysticism; or by William Byrd's half-Catholic, half-Protestant sacred works, jealously protected and nurtured through centuries of neglect in the chapels and vaulted libraries of this unusual university city of Oxford till their rediscovery and restitution after the Second World War. The Pope and the Archbishop could do a lot worse tonight than sit down together and immerse themselves in a rendering of Palestrina's *Missa Papae Marcelli*. I can think of no better way of demonstrating to them that despite their differences they were talking about the same God.

Christianity has many faces. It is expressed in many thousands of different ways. One of music's most potent attributes is that it is non-linguistic. Unlike the words of the scriptures or the Mass or even the Lord's Prayer, music does not need translation for it to spread across the planet. The trend we are currently witnessing in music, that of the cross-fertilization and intermingling of diverse styles, traditions, cultures to create new amalgamated styles — the rubbing of musical shoulders across the world — has been at work in sacred music ever since the first missionaries took their hymnals, full of rich European harmonies, to Africa. Anyone can listen to a choir singing the Kyrie Eleison and be moved by it: the fact that the words are idiomatic Ancient Greek is irrelevant to that transaction. Similarly, anyone can be swept away by the pulsating tribal energy of African ritual music, regardless of their ability to grasp the sung words.

All of the above reasons explain to some extent the extraordinary heritage of sacred music thus far, but given that this heritage is already bursting to the brim with music, why would one want to add to it now, in the year 2000? Surely we have enough settings of the Magnificat and the Mass by now. Surely the priorities and tastes of our modern society demand a fresh approach to religious observance, free from the baggage of our complicated European past? I will answer this by looking now at the motivation behind my writing sacred music.

My first reason is to do with what one might call a bridge of continuity. I started my musical life as a chorister, here in Oxford, as the son of parents who believed in the kind of education that included Christianity and its culture. The power of that culture seeped into my bones every day of my life at an impressionable age as I sang the music of Byrd, Bach or Britten. One reason I write sacred music is because it is in my blood.

Two years ago I made a TV series about choral singing around the world. In the course of the filming I spent many hours interviewing the cathedral choristers at Christ Church, trying to find out from them what they liked or disliked about the experience. All of them, without exception, declared that the best thing about it was the beauty of the music. Though they regretted, perhaps understandably, the amount of time they spent rehearsing (especially when compared to the free time activities of other children their age) they also knew that without it the standard of the singing would be low. For gifted children, underachievement in their chosen field is utterly debilitating. They are inspired and driven by a desire to perform at the highest level. The most interesting chat I had though, was with a boy who talked about the fact that boys just like him had been doing more or less the same as him in the same cathedral during the reign of Elizabeth I. This he found spooky but also rather brilliant. I identified strongly with his response. I too feel as if I am swimming in some immense cultural river whose source is way, way back, and between whose banks also flowed the composers and performers of a thousand-year story. The sense of the history of the tradition is invigorating to someone like myself at the very tail end of it, but also somewhat daunting. In my experience, challenges that are daunting are challenges worth doing. The gallery of famous names whose masterworks I have to follow do at any rate instil in me a sense of humility.

Music of all kinds can provide solace and comfort. For many people it fulfils this function in place of religion, of course, but when combined with the resonance of great sacred texts, it is doubly powerful. I am acutely aware of the fact that my setting of Psalm 23, originally composed as the theme music for *The Vicar of Dibley*, nice tune though it may be, is given depth and meaning by its text, and given hundreds of performances in churches all over Britain to boot. I am reminded of the funeral of Diana, Princess of Wales, at Westminster Abbey. The music played a crucial role in giving expression to people's feelings of grief and loss – and none more so than John Tavener's *Song for Athene* – a contemporary piece by a living composer, taking pride of place next to Verdi and Elton John. My view is that the recent resurgence in interest in Gregorian chant, in the moodily thoughtful religious music of Arvo Pärt, in Górecki and Tavener (sometimes dubbed composers of 'the new simplicity'), in CDs subtitled 'music of inner harmony' or 'music of spiritual oneness' and so on, is indicative of a deep, unspoken need. We live in a harsh, noisy culture; how surprising is it that sacred music, born of a much calmer frame of mind, should be enjoying something of a comeback? I am concerned at the increasing hostility (on television in particular) towards anything that is thoughtful, delicate, concentrated. Television is the universal mouthpiece and opinion-former for all Westernized societies, and yet slow-moving, meditative music that lasts longer than five minutes can find no place on it. Television is too impatient. This kind of music is invisible on television yet sought after by millions of people as an alternative, as a necessary form of comfort and solace. It is tempting to include religion in general in that description, but I am less convinced that religions are invisible on TV (some even have their own TV channels), and there is still so much anger, bigotry and bloodshed associated with the world's religions from Jerusalem to Londonderry that I am not sure even Christianity's image is wholly peaceful or comforting.

Sacred music is at its most potent when it is helping people come to terms with death. Several composers reached the pinnacle of their choral writing in their Requiems – Mozart, Berlioz, Verdi, Duruflé, Fauré and Britten come to mind. Perhaps I am unusual, but my favourite hymn is not the jubilant fanfare of 'Praise my soul the king of heaven' (stirring though it is) but the dark and foreboding 'Lead, kindly light, amid the encircling gloom'. Requiems and Passions are not, of course, for the dead but for the living. Their beauty and force suggest something bigger and more mysterious than the individual death. They seem to remind the grieving listener of their common humanity.

Finally, it is hard not to come to the conclusion, as a composer, that music is in some sense supernatural. I apologize for the word, since it conjures up *The Twilight Zone* and dotty clairvoyants, but it does approach the sense of something powerful that we do not really comprehend. Music's strange alchemy is a mystery. And it is my personal view that

Christianity is also a mystery. The two have formed so compelling a marriage over the last thousand or so years because a person standing in a church, chapel, cathedral or abbey who hears ethereal or uplifting music has a much stronger sense of something 'outside' their normal existence than if they are simply listening to a man discussing a passage from St Paul. Intelligent and perceptive as St Paul's thinking undoubtedly is, it is not magical. If you are expecting your flock to have faith in a man rising from the dead, a virgin birth, a host of totally implausible miracles, or the bodily transfer of God into an edible wafer, you will need stronger special effects up your sleeve than a man waving around some incense. Music, an abstract and elusive art that disarms one's emotional defences and saturates us in feeling and confusion, is almost the only thing we have left that can convey a majestic and disturbing mystery.

Western music, broadly speaking, began with Pythagoras and his concept of it being the earthly manifestation of the 'music of the spheres' – celestial music being reflected or ricocheted down to humankind from above. Throughout the Middle Ages, the Church adopted this notion, neatly modifying it to mean the Christian God and the heavenly angels beaming down to us their perfect, divine sound, an echo of which we meekly picked up as if on a transmitter. Composers described their art as dictating God's music. Like Pythagoras, they claimed to have a direct link to the heavenly soundbank. Music, even as late as the Renaissance, was a glimpse of the perfection of heaven. As the Baroque period dawned, a new role for music began to coexist with the old, namely that its job was to portray a human's emotions and therefore to help him or her relate to them. In Shakespeare's plays we see the two ideas of music – as a heavenly, mystical property or as a human, illustrative art – cropping up side by side. Prospero's island in *The Tempest* is a magical arena of musical sound that no one quite understands, and yet in *Twelfth Night* music is commandeered by a duke merely to provide the right set-up for courtship ('If music be the food of love . . .'). The first of the towering baroque composers, Claudio Monteverdi, considered sacred music and secular music to be virtually indistinguishable (the opening of his 1610 *Vespers* and his opera *L'Orfeo* of 1607 use identical music). Man's music and God's music are no longer separable.

For the next 350 years music primarily portrayed humankind's joy, suffering, love, death and ecstasy. Even Bach's Passions are focused on Jesus Christ's agony as a man rather than as a manifestation of God. Only when Olivier Messiaen began talking about his compositions as mystical creations reflecting God's glory in the 1940s and 1950s was this role for music challenged. He started a movement to redefine the potential and meaning of music, a movement that is now in full sway. Arvo Pärt and John Tavener have been his most famous lieutenants in this trend. Though I am a commercial, practical composer who sees myself as more artisan than shaman, I too subscribe to the view that music may have a transcendent power beyond our normal understanding. I will give you the reason why I believe this.

Four years ago I was staying with friends in a small village, Tourettes-sur-Loup, on the French Côte d'Azur, composing for six hours a day and enjoying myself the rest of the time. One week in August, while transcribing the fair copy of one of my musicals, my work on it was interrupted. I woke very early one morning at around 6 o'clock and had the overwhelming feeling there was a new piece lurking at the back of my mind – not just a fragment or echo of it but a whole work – a Magnificat for choir and organ. My first reaction, lying awake in bed that morning, was to wonder if it had in fact already been written by someone else and I was merely remembering a piece I used to sing or play. This is nearly always my first instinct on 'discovering' a new piece in my head. My second reaction was one of surprise, since I had no commissions outstanding to provide a Magnificat and Nunc Dimittis for anyone, but I did have a splitting headache. How had the music implanted itself there if it was (a) uncalled for and (b) having to compete with the after-effects of some rather heavy Provençal wine? I got up, listening to the piece running through from beginning to end a number of times (to check that it was all there) and decided to walk the mile or so to the village for the morning bread, in the hope that I might clear the headache. During the walk I found that the entire Magnificat was there, intact, and that it didn't seem to have been borrowed from another composer. I thought of musical directors or choirs who might want a Magnificat. I had a delicious bowl of coffee and croissant and read *Nice Matin*. My next thought was whether there was a Nunc Dimittis to go with the Magnificat. I started back towards the house, baguettes under arm, and sure enough, the Nunc Dimittis began 'transmitting' itself, as if it had always been there and I simply hadn't summoned it up from the appropriate filing cabinet. By the time I arrived back at the house, now completely knackered and overheated and with no sign of the headache subsiding, the Nunc Dimittis was safely embedded in my head. By supper that night both pieces were on manuscript paper and by breakfast the next morning I had persuaded Robin Nelson of Marlborough College that his excellent chamber choir needed a new set of Evening Canticles.[2]

I do not in all honesty know where that music comes from in its virtually finished form. The way it appears unprompted in my head without warning or effort is baffling. Is it just a chemical reaction? Is it a dream conjured up by my subconscious in the middle of the night, amalgamating all the music I have drifting about in my brain into a recognizable shape? Was this piece always in me, but needed coaxing out? I cannot articulate this mystery without fumbling around for words; who or what is feeding me this music? But it is undoubtedly a mystery. My suspicion is that this music is coming from the same place or spiritual dimension that gave birth to the music I adore in other composers. The nature of the genesis of my music suggests to me that sacred music, in particular, has something most unusual and special to offer us. We need it as we needed it in the bush and cave. We need some connection with the non-physical forces around us, and music can make that connection. That seems to me to be a good reason to write sacred music. It is a magnificent mystery.

As for the future, music has always been, and is always going to be, the handmaiden of worship and prayer. What I am less certain about is the form that that music will take. I hope very much that the melting pot of different styles and traditions that coexist in modern Britain will be encouraged to thrive, that the various branches will prosper alongside one another and not be forced into a conflict where only one prevails. I am adamant that excellence has been the driving force of all areas of sacred music in the past and will continue to be so. While I admire and applaud the easily mastered and enjoyed Taizé chants, I wish those who use them would make that extra small effort and sing in tune. While I unfashionably adore the Psalms sung to Victorian chants, I yearn for the text to be clearly and conscientiously delivered, as if the words mattered. While I appreciate the joyous clamour made by a drum kit, I wish drummers would in turn appreciate the acoustics of an old stone church and make some space for all the other joyous sounds within. While I, notoriously, relish the sight of a great organ as much as the next anorak, I would be only too happy, from time to time, to hear instead instrumental ensembles played with panache and commitment.

From a purely personal perspective, the unique choral tradition nurtured over several centuries in Britain has been an inspiration. I hope in the decades to come it is allowed to develop a sense of the contemporary and accessible without losing its integrity. What this means in practice is that a respect for Palestrina is as important as having a great, singable melody; that a sympathy with the performance techniques required for Purcell will enrich the performing of Britten; and that being aware of the rhythmic possibilities of popular music and the harmonic complexities of Rachmaninov never did anyone any harm.

3

God, Theology and Music

JAMES MACMILLAN

There has been a resurgence of interest in a particular kind of contemporary music in recent years. This has been a surprise to many, especially the composers involved, because we live at the end of a century that has seen a retreat by the composing community from the larger music-loving public. If we look back to the early days of the century we see figures like Schoenberg, establishing private societies for the performance of contemporary music. A perception is beginning to emerge within the composing community that the priorities of composers have in some way separated from the priorities of the larger music-loving public. At the very time when a museum culture was beginning to be the main priority of classical music listeners, composers were going into a very exploratory mode. In the century of the Holocaust and the loss of meaning generally, composers went into a kind of laboratory phase when the very nature of music was the stuff of their investigations. Composers like Boulez, Stockhausen, Berio and the young Turks of the post-war generation took music into a very abstract phase indeed by making explorations into the purely abstract nature of music but with an ideological and idealistic desire to turn their backs on the past. They wanted to start afresh from year zero, as it were, to write a music that was untainted by tradition, a music that would not have any resonance of a failed bourgeois culture.

However, in the last 15 years or so a number of composers

have bucked this trend. Composers such as John Tavener, Henryk Górecki and Arvo Pärt have been taken into the affections of a larger music-loving public, not always the traditional older classical music audience but a new audience of younger people. Some might say disparagingly that it is a 1990s new age audience that has taken to the mysticism and the simplicities of the likes of Tavener, Górecki and Pärt. Why are we seeing such a flourishing of spiritual composers at this time? The music of these three composers on the face of it is very beautiful; it is music that avoids the complexities common in a lot of contemporary, avant-garde, modernist music of the twentieth century. There is a return to some sense of modality, if not tonality, and there is an ethereal atmosphere in their music that I think makes people relax and feel vaguely spiritual. There seems to be a hunger for something to fill the spiritual void and some of this music at least gives people a kind of folk memory of what spiritual sustenance was about.

Music and spirituality are very closely entwined. They have a centuries-long relationship and you could say that music is the most spiritual of the arts. More than the other arts, I think, music seems to get into the crevices of the human–divine experience. Music has the power to look into the abyss as well as to the transcendent heights. It can spark the most severe and conflicting extremes of feeling and it is in these dark and dingy places where the soul is probably closest to its source where it has its relationship with God, that music can spark life that has long lain dormant. I haven't included my own name in this list of popular spiritual composers for various reasons, but the one thing we do have in common is a love of ancient church music and a desire to look back at the ancient tradition of Christian music and especially Gregorian Chant, which I am always using in my music: I quote chant, I allude to it, I fragment it, I dissect it, I use it as the building blocks, the DNA, of larger structures. It obviously means a lot to me. It is a kind of perfect music. I also feel I am rooting myself in something very deep culturally and spiritually. I feel I am plugging into a rich seam because not only is Gregorian Chant the most perfect music melodically, it is also the music that singly most characterizes Catholic musical tradition and which carries the liturgy and theology behind the chant. I nearly always have a pre-musical reason for wanting to compose but that is now a rather odd position to hold, because music, as well as being the most spiritual of the arts, is also the most abstract of the arts. Much twentieth-century music has retreated into itself, and many composers have become more and more obsessed, perhaps in the manner of trainspotters, with the very substance, the very stuff of music. They have tended to divorce themselves from the possibility of music having resonances and connections with life outside music. Music has this facility to retreat into itself. But perhaps I should speak subjectively about my own experiences as a younger composer.

When I was studying in university environments there was an attitude among my fellow composers that music was all about the notes on the page and the way one moves those notes about the page in as clever a way as possible. Anything else was extraneous and irrelevant. Music was complete in itself and need not have any extra-musical reason for its existence. This disturbed me quite a lot although, as a composer, I shared their attitudes, looking at the nature of music, trying to get to grips with the techniques of composition, the very stuff of music and how to build its structures and its designs successfully. Yet I did have other interests. For example, I was very interested in what I describe as the vernacular forms of music, music that exists outside the European tradition of serious art. I had played in a rock band when I was a teenager. In my twenties I had sung and played in traditional Scottish and Irish folk bands in clubs and pubs in the West of Scotland. Here was a very different kind of music with a very different kind of musician fulfilling a social function not of the art tradition.

They were different from my composer friends who for one reason or another were distanced from vernacular forms of music; there was no connection between these two worlds or these two sets of friends. I was also very interested in politics and had prematurely joined a political party when I was 14. I was involved in various humanitarian activities of an ideological and idealistic nature and this world seemed to have no intersection with the world of composition. Yes, my fellow composers were romantically revolutionary but that's not the same thing as being practically engaged in the world of politics from an idealistic position. And there was another world, a world I shared with my fellow Papes who came together for the practice of the faith. Catholicism has always meant a lot to me but even in those early days I couldn't see any way of allowing the religious dimension into the practice of my music and, of course, those who flattered themselves that they were at the cutting edge of this particular art form would say that there was no place for something as reactionary and as anachronistic as the Catholic faith in a modernist artistic world.

So you can see a number of compartments of my life emerging here that had no intersection or connection whatsoever and it led to a rather schizophrenic existence. Yet I took it for granted that that was the way it had to be and I saw no real possibility of allowing my music to reflect these other things in this severe and rigorous abstract expression. I remember looking with some envy at friends in the other arts – writers, film makers, poets and visual artists – who were inspired by these same things and who were able to give space and dimension in their work to a resonance of the world about them, either the physical or the political world or in some cases the metaphysical world. These experiences seemed to be off-bounds to me and my fellow composers. Now, whether something has changed in the Zeitgeist in the last fifteen years or whether it was just a process of maturation on my part, I began to see the barriers, which divide these compartments starting to dissolve, with strong possibilities of one element cross-fertilizing with another. For example, I allowed my interest in vernacular music forms to infuse the processes of artistic creation in my work as a serious composer. And I began to see possibilities of allowing the political dimension some space in my compositions and ultimately I began to see really strong possibilities of allowing a spiritual dimension to emerge within my work as a composer.

The first piece that allowed me to do this was a music theatre piece called *Busqueda*, a Spanish word meaning 'search'. It is a setting of poems by the Mothers of the Disappeared from Argentina interlaced with the Latin text of the Mass. When I found these poems I was struck by their emotional power and the fact that, while they did not constitute sophisticated literature, they were nevertheless extremely moving and had a transformative effect on those who read them. These women poets provoked something angry, fierce, loving, hopeful and grief-stricken, yet they would not have written any poetry had they not been the Mothers of the Disappeared. I was also struck by the simple and traditional faith lying behind the poems. I think what I wanted to do in this piece was to bring together the timeless and the contemporary, the secular and the sacred, the religious and the political. I am intrigued, for example, by the dialogue between the message of the Gospels and the message of various idealistic political responses in our own time. I have always been intrigued by the engagement between politics and religion: the conflicts and contradictions between them and also the synthesis of ideas that sometimes emerge. This piece *Busqueda* and another piece called *Cantos Sagrados*, a setting of poems by Ariel Dorfman and others, again interlaced with Latin liturgical texts, were my first attempts to make perceptible connections between the musical and the extra-musical, the religious and the political, and I describe these two pieces, naively, as being inspired by the basic principles of Liberation Theology.[2]

A piece that I wrote a few years after *Busqueda* called *The Confession of Isobel Gowdie* was inspired by the story of a woman who seemed to represent the outsider in our midst and the way that outsiders always seem to succumb to our hatred.[3] She was a woman convicted of witchcraft in late seventeenth-century Scotland who made a fantastical confession and suffered brutally at the hands of her tormentors. I wanted to write a piece of music that on one level made some kind of statement of solidarity with this archetypal figure. But my choice of this particular archetype was similar to my choice of the Disappeared as archetypes because, in their lives and in their experiences of hatred and death and rejection, they resonate with the original archetype of Christ in the Passion narrative. I think there is an ethical dimension behind the composition of *The Confession of Isobel Gowdie*, but many musicians would regard this as contentious. It sits uneasily with the view that music should be complete in itself and not have deeper representational resonances with extra-musical issues.

It is often said of Tavener's music that it is a celebration of the risen Christ. Whereas many have said about my music that I seem to be much more preoccupied with the crucified Christ, that I seem to be drawn again and again to the Passion. I think this is true and it may account for the ideological difference between myself and the likes of Tavener and also our technical and aesthetic differences in style and approach. Yes, I am drawn by the sacrificial aspect of the great Christian narrative and I do seem to be going round and round the same three days of history. The fact is that if history had to be changed, if we had to be changed, then God had to interact with us in a severe way. You can't have the resurrection without the crucifixion. In a number of the composers I have mentioned there is a sense of the transcendent, which is beautiful, but there is also a deliberate avoidance of conflict in their work. They deliberately, aesthetically and technically avoid the whole notion of conflict. Tavener, for example, has stated that he has turned his back on that aspect of the Western canon. Symphonic form and sonata form are now anathema to him because they are about pitting widely contrasted materials against each other so that they come together, inter-act, clash, fuse and develop like a storyteller with climaxes and conflicts. I am attracted to that in Beethoven and Mozart as in Tippett and in a lot of modernist music of our own time. My character needs that sense of conflict. In purely musical terms I need to tell a story; I need to create dramas and the best stories are the ones that have resolutions of conflict, not just resolution, while a lot of recent so-called spiritual music can be a mono-dimensional experience of transcendence without a sense of sacrifice. In my *Vigil* Symphony, influenced by the day before Easter, the first movement is called Light, but has some of the darkest music I have ever written because I don't think we can see the light until we can know why there is light, and that involves a knowledge of the dark. Will I ever tire of circling the same three days in history? I don't think so; it's too rich a seam.

Michael Symmons Roberts, whose poetry I have set a lot, has used the term 'the deep mathematics of creation' about music. This is a term that chimes with me because music does seem to be a kind of calculus, a means of calculating some-thing of our very nature. And because we are made in the image of God, music can be seen as a calculus of the very face of God. One way of doing that in music is to circle round the very moments when God made his deepest interaction with human history. I think that is why I'm drawn back obsessively to these three days. I can't help it; I know that the answer might be there. With this form of musical calculus there is an attempt to open doors and encounter the face of God. The face of God would be an awesome sight, if we could ever see it with human eyes and the way of finding access to that awe and fear is to experience God through the death and resurrection of his Son. Perhaps this is the reason I have drawn on quite frightening instances of human activity in our own time and within our cultural memory, such as Isobel Gowdie and the Mothers of the Disappeared. Here you are encountering the crucifixion narrative afresh in the lives of ordinary people. So even if there is a political dimension to their stories, it is like a mirror image or resonance of the great archetypal story of Christ. And to avoid the darkness and the tragedy is to refuse to face up to the abyss, which is our human experience. It is a flight from reality and from the true nature of God. Spirituality is not just some sort of easily won feel-good factor. Spirituality is something that you find in the here-and-now, in the fears, aspirations, joys and tragedies of human life, in the grit and mire of daily existence, which then raises incredible possibilities of compassion in those encounters.

Being a composer I am frequently asked to speak about my music. Inevitably the question of inspiration arises. How did the ideas come? What made you think of that? How do you start formulating your ideas? These questions are deceptively simple and yet frighteningly enormous. They rank alongside the 'meaning of life' question in their ability to inspire terror and humility in any composer rash enough to attempt a response. Most of the time it's easy to hide behind answers which tackle the abstract nature of music. Most composers, myself included, devise methods of channelling attention towards impressive-looking charts complete with complicated note rows, Fibonacci series and Schenkerian-style structural analyses.

Music is, after all, the most abstract of all the arts. At a fundamental level it needs no point of reference beyond itself, other than its own substance, its own methodology and technique, its own explicable parameters. And yet these questions, whether posed externally or internally, keep coming. During a recent television interview the somewhat acerbic host, Muriel Gray, proffered one such question. Recognizing that spirituality was now an issue of current debate again in the discussion of a lot of contemporary music, she was nevertheless keen to explore the matter from her own secular perspective. Did I, as a composer, think that religious piety sat uncomfortably with freedom of artistic expression? Did I not think that the greatest artistic challenges were faced from within a spiritual void involving a struggle which relied on no emotional or religious crutches, thus the artist could forge his or her own sense of meaning without falling back on any received traditional (and therefore probably false) sense of meaning?

As a semi-automatic response the words 'divine inspiration' slipped unguarded from my lips and were sitting there, exposed and vulnerable, awaiting the inevitable avalanche to be heaped upon them. It failed to materialize. My interrogator was surprised by my response, which she described as non-conformist and, in its own way, avant-garde. Then it struck me that the engagement between theology and culture, between religion and the arts is now such a faded memory for most people that a whole generation has grown up without an understanding of the true meaning and implication in the word 'inspiration'. And when a creative person comes across this definition for the first time, it is a discovery made with undisguised delight – a recognition of a primal truth that has lain hidden for a long time.

The true spiritual meaning of words like inspiration and transformation has been obscured by the layers of transient trendiness which pass for much cultural debate nowadays. A childlike pleasure accompanies the realization that inspiration, from the Latin *inspiratio*, means 'in-breathing', an arousal or infusion of an impulse or illumination that impels a person to speak, act or write under the influence of some creative power. Divine inspiration is understood as the charismatic supernatural influence that moved and guided the prophets of the Old Testament in revealing God's will to Israel and the attendant writing of the word. The Christian tradition understands that the Spirit of God has been profoundly involved in the actions and communication of these prophets and authors.

Over the years I have scanned scripture from a composer's perspective looking for clues as to the true nature of human creativity, of artistic fecundity, clues as to the significance of the eternal interaction between the human and the divine, clues to the religious artist about the significance of the full and active engagement of all one's human faculties – the cerebral, the aesthetic, the critical, the emotional, the visceral, the carnal and the corporeal; clues as to how all this should be open to the will of God; clues as to how one can become a channel for the divine will, without diminishing one's own God-given free will.

Some of these clues may be unveiled in a couple of crucial passages from scripture. In Genesis, God presents his limitless love for humanity in the gift of creation yet, at the same time invites Adam, the archetype, to make his own sense of this new world. God provokes Adam into calling on his, that is Adam's, own imagination in naming the constituent elements of his world. Humanity's inner creativity is being *inspired* to express itself in the face of God's immeasurable love (Genesis 2.18–23). Here is the interaction, indeed it might be suggested, the interface of God's will with that of human beings.

The creativity implied in the story of Adam's rib has many resonances for composers who, through the centuries, have always taken fragments of material, consciously or unconsciously, from elsewhere and breathed new life into them, creating new forms, new avenues and structures of expression. Whether these fragments are taken from liturgy, from plainsong, from folk song, from self-quotation, from allusions to other sources, from traditional cadential formulae, from half-remembered melodic shape, from a dimly perceived harmonic resonance, from a distant pulse of rhythm – they are all like embers of an old fire, extracted and gathered up, and wafted into a new flame. Indeed one of my own pieces is entitled

Adam's Rib (1994–5)[4] and is simply an acknowledgement of this eternally regenerative process of music as it develops through the ages, 'This at last is bone of my bones and flesh of my flesh.'

An even more crucial New Testament passage from St Luke is linked, like a mirror image, with the extract from Genesis, through a text, by Jeremy Taylor (1613–67), that I once set for choir and organ – *On the Annunciation of the Blessed Virgin Mary* (Reginald Heber, 1822).[5]

> How good a God have we, who, for our sake,
> To save us from the burning lake,
> Did change the order of creation;
> At first he made
> Man like himself in his own image, now
> In the more blessed reparation
> The Heavens bow:
> Eternity took the measure of a span,
> And said,
> 'Let us like ourselves make man
> And not from man the woman take,
> But from the woman, man.'

In St Luke's account of the annunciation, it is not just Mary's fecundity that is inspiring to a creative person. A more powerful and more pertinent metaphor for the religious artist is the balance between, on the one hand, Mary's independent free will and, on the other, her openness to the power of the Holy Spirit. There is something in the instinct of an artist or a composer, or any creative person, or any Christian for that matter, which is inexorably drawn to the idea of Mary's 'vesselship' – the notion of making oneself as a channel for the divine will. This is not, of course, to negate the individual's human will. The incarnation came about through Mary's free and rational acceptance of God's plan for her. Similarly an artist or a composer who thinks in real and meaningful terms of a divine inspiration would be mistaken in underestimating the full and active participation of all one's human faculties. It is a mistake to negate our human dimension and experience. It is through the interaction of all that makes us human – our intellect, our intelligence, our emotion and our physicality, our universal experience of joy and despair, our flesh and blood – with the breath of God which brings forth creative fruit (for an artist new work, new art, new music). Jesus himself was at once flesh of Mary *and* the Son of God.

This is why many have said that to be an artist, to be a Christian in fact, is to be spiritually or paradigmatically female. The Dominican, Gilbert Márkus, sees this in the marriage-motif of the New Testament, in which the Bride makes herself ready for the coming of the Groom. '[This] is the sexual and reproductive metaphor of God's relationship with humanity, both collectively and individually. The [ultimate] paradigm here is Mary, whose son is also the Son of God.'[6] Mary who was receptive to God; Mary who was filled by God; Mary who bore God's son. Mary is the paradigm of our receptivity. Mary is an extreme version of all of us – a model for all creative people, an image for Christian educators and an example for all Christian believers. The Christian believer is paradigmatically female: receptive to the seed of God's word. Receptive of the potency of God, the believer is waiting to be filled, longing to bear the fruit which will result from his or her union with God, to bring Christ to birth in our own life stories.

We come closest to Mary's example of receptivity, longing and patient openness to God in our own religious contemplations. For these silent, introspective searches we are required to give up time. Prayer and contemplation are undeniably a kind of sacrifice. That is why we are so reluctant to put time aside. There is even at the heart of most committed Christians, the fear of inspiration since, on this view of inspiration, there is an implicit invitation to relinquish control of our time, of our structures, of our selves. Inspiration, in this sense, need not be associated with any particular form of liturgy and worship, nor need it be seen as the prerogative of particular groups of Christians who have the bounty of exclusive means of communication with God. Instead it may be regarded as an acceptance of our potential to be stretched, deepened, challenged and changed. The very notion that human beings may be changed embodies a sacrifice of some part of the self; the self that exists at this moment and with whom 'I' might be comfortable will, inevitably, be altered. The fear that this realization induces, however dimly perceived, is an entirely understandable phenomenon. In the annunciation it is clear that Luke regards Mary as embodying both fear of the unknown as well as the recognition that change is inevitable. Mary's 'blessedness', like Hannah's (1 Samuel 1.16ff.), is bound up in her preparedness to be open to God. Again, as Luke has it, her soul magnifies the Lord and her spirit rejoices in God.

We know that her response to the annunciation was an inspired and radical vision of a new life, a new revolutionary moral universe. We see this in the Canticle of Mary, the Magnificat, where, as a good Jewish girl, she was able to take the words of Isaiah and transform them into her own vision: a vision in which the world as we know it is turned upside down, inside out; where the proud are scattered; where the mighty are deposed; where the poor are exalted and the rich and powerful are turned on their heels. Through the breath of God Mary is inspired to see a new world. Her eyes are opened to a frighteningly radical overturn of everything that is accepted – an end to tyranny and oppression. The world is changed through Mary's vision. Through Mary's example we learn to see beyond the apparently obvious and predetermined past of human behaviour. In Mary's example we see that when the breath of God moved through her she was made 'God-like' in her potential to love.

The patristic writers talked about *deificatio* in connection with the breath of God, in that its influence makes us divine. We begin to see things like God, to behave like God, like Adam when he engaged his inspired imagination to name the animals and other things in the Garden. The breath of God becomes our breath. No wonder we are terrified of being changed by our contemplations. Because along with the unbelievably joyous upheaval in Mary's life, the annunciation also brought the shadow of the cross. The recognition, right at the heart of Luke's infancy narrative, is that all joys carry their own ambiguity – that our soul will be pierced by a sword (Luke 2.35).

Music also demands our time. It unfolds its narratives in time with an authority that will not be hurried. Something essential to our lives is sacrificed to music. Whether we are performers, composers or listeners we need to give something up, something of ourselves, something of our humanity, our 'flesh and blood' – our time – to learn its intricacies, to communicate its depths in performance, or in its very inception itself – and in our serious hearing of it. Being openly receptive to the transforming power of music is analogous to the patient receptivity to the divine that is necessary for religious contemplation.

I have for a long time seen music as a striking analogy for God's relationship with us. As John McDade has it, 'Music may be the closest human analogue to the mystery of the direct and effective communication of grace.'[7] I would go further and suggest that music is a phenomenon connected to the work of God because it invites us to touch what is deepest in our souls, and to release within us a divine force. Music opens doors to a deepening and broadening of understanding. It invites connections between organized sound and lived experience or suspected possibilities. In the connection is found the revelation, a realization of something not grasped before. Such 'seeing' offers revelations about human living and divine relationships that can effect changes in our choices, our activities and our convictions. Music allows us to see, like Mary, beyond to what lurks in the crevices of the human–divine experience.

Rowan Williams, in a sermon for the Three Choirs Festival, said:

> To listen seriously to music and to perform it are among our most potent ways of learning what it is to live with and before God, learning a service that is a perfect freedom. No one and nothing can compel our contemplation, except the object in its own right. In this 'obedience' of listening and following, we are stretched and deepened, physically challenged as performers, imaginatively as listeners. The time we have renounced, given up, is given back to us as a time in which we have become more human, more real, even when we can't say what we have learned, only that we have changed.[8]

Mary learned to live with and before God. She was not commanded or forced from on high, but the breath of God entered her – and she was stretched, deepened, challenged and changed. As a composer asked about inspiration I am drawn back to these pages from Luke's Gospel. I find inspiration in Mary's Magnificat, which is one of the most set texts by composers throughout the ages, and in the story of the annunciation, apparently one of the most painted scenes of the scriptures. Artists are pointing us towards these two events in St Luke. There is obviously something momentously significant in their ubiquity throughout musical and artistic history. There is equally something momentously significant in Mary's central presence at the heart of these of these things. She is not only an example and a model for all Christianity but in this is the embodiment of what human beings experience only dimly; that we live with ambiguity of limitation and creative possibility in constant tension. She opens the door to the very heart of God, and in the silence of my own contemplation, in that necessary stillness where as all composers know that music mysteriously begins, the following words from our sacred liturgy have lodged themselves in the womb of my soul, trapped in a scarlet room, gestating gently with a tiny distant pulse:

Hail Mary, full of grace
The Lord is with thee
Blessed art thou among women
And blessed is the fruit of thy womb, Jesus.

4

Darkness to Light, Cycles and Circles:
The Sacred in My Music

ROBERT SAXTON

That music is capable of leading us from the mundane to a spiritual level has been a significant element in our culture since Plato and Pythagoras, but I think it important not to confuse the inherent ability of music as music to transcend the everyday, with the way in which those qualities may, or may not, be made manifest. With regard to the liturgical and the sacred, the *Oxford English Dictionary* gives the following definitions, among others: 'liturgical' – pertaining to the liturgy, public worship; 'sacred' – dedicated to a deity. What I have to say to you today is bound up with these two definitions. I would add that, for an artist, sacred can mean dedicated to a higher purpose, rather than, necessarily, to a deity in a specific sense.

I feel a close affinity with the Western musical tradition of goal-directed structures and composition as a process of transformation and argument, in the formal sense. Historically, this results from the development of harmonic counterpoint, local and long-range tension between consonance and dissonance and strong architecturally important cadences. In the later Renaissance, these developments produced liturgical music which, however contemplative it may sometimes appear to be, is a far cry from the homophonically articulated stasis of Eastern liturgical music, for example, whose influence is currently fashionable in certain quarters. My preoccupations over many years stem from this background and my Judaeo-Christian heritage. The title of this chapter mentions cycles and circles; in conjunction with this goes my fascination with moving, in my music, from darkness to light. In short, my music always creates a journey, but its harmonic and other structural processes beg the question as to whether we do, in fact, move towards a goal or whether, perhaps, all goes round in a circle in order to be reborn and begin again, bearing in mind that both Judaism and Christianity are goal-directed religions. In my own work, these are not concepts added on after, or during, composition; they are deeply embedded in the architectural/musical argument. Behind this are two types of liturgical observance with which I grew up: on the one hand, the Orthodox synagogue, with its rather static, elaborate, monophonic cantorial and choral music, and simultaneously, on the other, school assembly and Anglican services, enshrining a dynamic musical tradition, from the Lutheran chorale onwards. As examples of this I would point to two short pieces of mine: *The Child of Light* and *At the Round Earth's Imagined Corners*.[1] Both of these were written for what my predecessor at Worcester College, Oxford, Robert Sherlaw-Johnson, calls 'occasional liturgical use'. Both describe a path from darkness to light, or the hope of this. I view and hear them as part of my overall compositional voyage, as an integral part of my work and thinking. In other words, when I write music to be sung in church, I do not put on a 'different hat'.

An awareness on the part of artists, from the Renaissance onwards, of the essentially human in relation to the sacred and their ability to express this was, for three or four centuries, considered to be a remarkable manifestation of the human spirit; a glorious celebration of humankind's gift for combining rational thought and emotional depth. Michelangelo's 'Pietà', Monteverdi's *Vespers*, Donne's great poetic celebrations of both divine and human love and Bach's humanity in conjunction with the sacred in the two Passions are examples of the unity that lies behind the sometimes apparently irreconcilable worlds of the secular and the sacred. I may be generalizing, but this can be summed up by saying that the symbolic gave way to the realistic; that is put bluntly, but Western painting, followed eventually by Western music, became capable of expressing the human–divine relationship in a unique manner. In our supposedly postmodern world, some now flirt with the non-Western and the archaic, placing the occidental heritage as just another item on a shelf in our cultural supermarket. I do not say this in a negative spirit, but I am concerned that 'the baby may go out with the bathwater'. For my own part, I cannot conceive of liturgical art (in whatever medium) in a 'decontextualized' way. By the same token I can see no value in liturgical art which is influenced by commercial factors and short-term ends.

The idea that art, particularly religious art, can be 'of its time' without being what one might call 'stylistically secular' or historically self-conscious was finely addressed by the great art historian E. H. Gombrich as follows:

Travellers in Italy in the 19th Century stood entranced in front of the frescoes of Giotto and enjoyed what they took to be an expression of a better age; indeed, a paradise of innocence. Consider the introduction of the chapter on Giotto in Lord Lindsay's *Sketches of the History of Christian Art* of 1846: 'The period we have now to deal with is one, comparatively speaking, of repose and tranquillity . . . the storm sleeps and the winds are still . . . there is in truth a holy purity, an innocent naïveté, a child-like grace and simplicity, a yearning after all things truthful, lovely and of good report . . . which few of the most perfect works of the mature era can boast of.'

Gombrich concludes:

You need not be an historian to recognise in this dream a complete figment of the author's imagination. The period of Giotto was also that of Dante, when the streets of Florence resounded with the clash between the Guelphs and the Ghibellines and the exiled poet painted a fearful picture of the wicked goings on in his native city. No wonder that I have so little patience with the notion that the style of art expresses the spirit of the age. There never was an age to match the majesty of Giotto's paintings.[2]

Gombrich is not suggesting that Giotto stepped outside his epoch in any sense (no artist can do so); he is not making out that Giotto craved an ideal, or idealized artistic past; that was left to a later age. He is, rather, praising Giotto's unswerving vision at the service of a strong idea. Nobody listening to a late Haydn quartet could seriously claim to hear the thunder of the French Revolution. In the twentieth century, Stravinsky and Messiaen achieved a ritualistic grandeur and contemplative stasis in their sacred works, but devoid of any sense of historical yearning or archaism. (Stravinsky's stylistic modelling has nothing to do with cultural nostalgia.) Both composers reinvented and reinvigorated in their own epoch; I shall return to this matter later.

Art of its time that aspires to a higher purpose is not a form of escapism. The latter seems to me to be a symptom of a 'late', nostalgic culture and that is something entirely different. Here is Gombrich again: 'We need not doubt that pre-Raphaelite painters such as Holman Hunt felt particularly sincere in rejecting such theatricalities and sensualities as displayed in some art; what is relevant is only their dubious conviction that the earlier Italians, such as Fra Angelico, may have lacked the technical mastery of later periods but were, for that very reason, more sincere than Raphael.' Technical mastery can, in itself, be an indication of a desire to achieve perfection at every level and I cannot think of any real artist who has not tried to achieve it. One has only to read Van Gogh's letters, or study Beethoven's sketches, to see what I mean.

Technical aspirations can, in themselves, be manifestations of high ideals, and equating naive simplicity with sincerity (or the reverse) is unwise. I am certain that Galileo, Descartes and Newton were driven to their discoveries by the same vision and desire to understand the universe as that which acts upon artists. Einstein encapsulated this in a speech at a dinner for Max Planck's sixtieth birthday in 1918:

> The supreme task of the physicist is to arrive at the universal elementary laws from which the cosmos can be built up by pure deduction. There is no logical path to these laws; only intuition, resting on sympathetic understanding can lead to them . . . the longing to behold harmony, is the source of the inexhaustible patience and perseverance with which Planck has devoted himself . . . to the most general problems of our science . . . [T]he state of mind that enables a person to do work of this kind is akin to that of the religious worshipper or the lover; the daily effort comes from no deliberate intention or programme, but straight from the heart.[3]

Note that Einstein uses the words 'religious worshipper' and 'lover' in this speech; he did so because he understood the essence of stretching both the imagination and the logical mind at the service of a much greater Idea, and that is very much Idea with a capital 'I' as Schoenberg meant it in his collection of essays *Style and Idea*. Sir Roger Penrose, Rouse Ball Professor of Mathematics in Oxford University, wrote the following in his book *The Emperor's New Mind*, about the great physicist, Paul Dirac: 'Dirac is unabashed in his claim that it was his keen sense of beauty that enabled him to divine his equation for the electron, while others had searched in vain'.[4] Forgive me for not defining beauty; I am not a professional aesthetician or philosopher, but what is clear is that both quotations display an awareness which goes well beyond the science laboratory. They acknowledge a state of wonder about, and gratitude for, our role as thinking, feeling beings within the created universe.

This generalized situation becomes specific in terms of music when the secular and sacred come into the picture as definitions or categories. Suppose that I claimed that Beethoven's late opus 132 quartet is, somehow, less religious (in the broadest sense) than Byrd's *Haec Dies*. I would argue that both are examples of supremely inspired work combined with faultless technical achievement; Byrd's inspiration manifests itself in an orthodox liturgical context, Beethoven's does not. This is not to say that Byrd was not impelled to write great music by his faith and the nature of the words (we know he was because he said so), but I would be wary about describing Beethoven's quartet as secular, particularly in our current cultural climate. It is not liturgical, but I hope that I have made it clear already that the liturgical, for many artists, may only be a specific way of focusing ideas and feelings which are made manifest in other ways in non-liturgical work. One of the movements of the Beethoven quartet is, after all, a wordless hymn of thanksgiving to the creator for recovery from illness. In 1973 I was present as a student at a lecture during which the Hungarian composer György Ligeti was asked if he thought music could be political. His answer was wise. He explained that, as a Jewish teenager in the late 1930s in Hungary, he had heard marching music with Nazi words; at the time of the 1956 uprising in Hungary, he witnessed the same music with a text praising the Communist Party. The music itself, he pointed out, certainly caused a crowd to feel patriotic, even militant, but any specific aim could only be made clear by the text. The relationship between text and music is a complex one and it is vital for any composer to consider whether or not the text being set is one familiar to the congregation, or not. This matter goes right across the spectrum, from audibility or words to unfamiliarity and expressive intention. Only one of the two short choral works that I have mentioned has a well-known text and, even in this case, it is not a liturgical text sung daily or weekly.

This problem was one which faced me directly in 1994, when I was asked to write a choral/orchestral piece for the Cambridge University Musical Society, in memory of my former Director of Studies at Cambridge, Dr Peter le Huray. He tried above all things to guide his students towards rational thought, reasonable behaviour (in the best sense) and to question rather than to accept. Knowing that the performance was to be in King's College Chapel, I wanted to pay tribute to Peter's intelligent wisdom in a religious context, but without using traditional texts. Eventually, I chose Lucretius (an extract about light from *De Rerum Natura*) and writings about light (in Latin) by Sir Isaac Newton (from his *Opticks*) for a piece called *Canticum Luminis*. Newton, after all, had conducted his experiments a few hundred yards from where the performance was to take place. In this case, my aim was to write a piece which was, in the broadest sense, religious and I made a conscious effort to 'remind' the audience of more traditional settings by setting Latin words concerned with light. I did not, in any way, alter my musical language. I was able to write my own music while being, if you like, referential in a wider sense and in relation to a specific tradition and a special building. There is no question that Newton worked with religious fervour at his scientific tasks and, indeed, spent more time at his desk writing about religion than he did about physics.

Music as part of ritual is as old as the human race and this leads me to consider the difference between an audience and a congregation. The latter is in attendance for the purpose of worship, the former not so. However, that is not to say that there is no difference between an audience which wishes to hear a string quartet play late Haydn and Bartok and those who go to a rock musical. I am not being judgemental here, merely realistic. Late Haydn quartets display a quality of thought and a remarkable balance between the worldly (even 'earthy') and the spiritually sustaining which emanates from a tradition which has, alas, come to be known as 'High Art'. It is a short step from the concert room to the church for Haydn, a fact demonstrated by his composition *The Seven Last Words from the Cross*, not a choral work but a string quartet.

We should consider also the strange case of Wagner, composing *Parsifal*, a supposedly religious drama for his own theatre, in order to support his obsessions concerning the Grail and redemption through love. Is the Bayreuth audience just that, an audience, or is it a 'cult congregation'? If so, what is it worshipping? Is a performance of *Parsifal* a ritual in any sense? I think not; a sacred drama it is, but exactly what is sacred about it, I am uncertain. It is a drama, I will grant it that. I put this to you for consideration; if by so doing, I emphasize the complexity of the issue as to what may, or may not, be religious/spiritual in and about art, and who may listen or observe, let alone worship, I will, to some extent, have succeeded. Spiritual and intellectual sustenance certainly exist in concert music, just as there exists liturgical music which has neither quality. I certainly do not have a simple answer to this multilayered picture. The story of Handel raging at the man who had the temerity to describe *Messiah* as entertainment to his face illustrates the point nicely. We are, to put it bluntly, faced with the issue of the artist's *intention* and *realization* of that intention, particularly regarding where and when a piece is to be performed.

Neither do the spiritual and religious aspects of creative work necessarily manifest themselves in a way that is conventionally ecclesiastical or liturgical. Britten's *Church Parables* (two of the three being based on biblical stories) are secular works specifically designed for church performance. Their sound-world is designed to suit places of Christian worship, both in terms of atmosphere and acoustically. They also combine the human and the spiritual in a direct way. In his Aspen Award speech in the USA in the 1960s, Britten complained about the fact that the radio had made it possible for a listener to switch off in the middle of Bach's *St Matthew Passion*, making the point that it was composed for a particular time during the church calendar. In essence, Britten was concerned about taking a work of art out of context. All of Messiaen's music is sacred and, as he put it, theological, but none of it (save *O Sacrum Convivium*) is liturgical. (The organ works can, of course, be played in a liturgical context.) It is, without doubt, some of the greatest religious music of the previous century. Why did a composer of this unforced originality and spiritual power not contribute significantly to the liturgical choral repertoire? He would have done so in a previous age. If the musical language is a problem I fail to see an easy solution. Perhaps he would have contributed had he had the advantages of the English Cathedral tradition and choir schools behind him. Who knows?

Manner of presentation can also affect a listener profoundly. Igor Stravinsky (a member of the Russian Orthodox Church) described Mozart's church compositions as 'sweets of sin'.[5] For him, the late Classical, dramatic style seemed inappropriate for church. Samuel Pepys, in his diary entry for 13 October 1663, condemned a synagogue service he attended in the City of London (Cromwell having allowed the Jewish community back into the country) as being too rowdy and lacking solemnity. Like Stravinsky, he expected a greater sense of solemn ritual than he observed. The other side of this coin, it seems to me, is the emergence of uninspired and uninspiring music for liturgical use which uses the trappings of the commercial musical world (and, frequently, the most clichéd elements of it). While moral issues and ethical values should, rightly, be considered more important than which translation of the Bible is employed during services, I believe, as a composer, that the manner in which worship is conducted does affect the worshipper and high standards, which are deeply interwoven with a living tradition, do fulfil the function of raising worship beyond the ordinary. If there is no attempt to scale the mountain, we may as well take the mountain away. Britten's frustration at the power we have been give to switch off a great work at will seems to me to impinge on the matter of the role of music in a liturgical context. Liturgical art is not a commodity.

The artist who makes religious pieces of work for church use does so out of a spiritual and sacred sense which may well not stem from conventional belief. Vaughan Williams wrote some of the greatest music of the twentieth century for the Anglican tradition, but he was an agnostic. Jacob Epstein, a New York Jew resident in Britain, made the wonderful 'Majestas' (a portrayal of Christ in majesty) for Llandaff Cathedral. I cite these examples to illustrate that we must beware of being naive in the area of sincerity. Gombrich's warning, which I cited earlier, is relevant. Conventional belief and sincerity (or, perhaps, a wrong-headed view of it) can be strange bedfellows where the arts are concerned, or are thought about simplistically.

I feel tradition as something living; I am no supporter of convention for its own sake, because it is static and unbending. Tradition, as I perceive it, is flexible and capable of transformation from within. Its strength lies in the power of its resonance across the centuries. When I go into a synagogue (particularly if it is an Orthodox one) I react in two ways: first, I feel like a stranger, because my Hebrew is very rusty and the ritual can seem mechanical; but, after a short time, I sense that I am part of something which is truly alive and beautiful and which speaks today. Yet it stretches back between three and five thousand years; that is a remarkable sensation, both emotionally and intellectually. In a Reform or Liberal synagogue, the ideas and manner of observance have changed, moved on, but the underlying sense of continuity and profundity remains. There is a parallel with the Church here, except that the Orthodox synagogue is, by and large, in the position that the Roman Catholic Church was prior to abandoning the use of Latin. I have, equally, always felt a sense of calm and inner peace when attending evensong in the Church of England and, for me as a musician, the choral tradition in this country has always meant a great deal. So, there is no conflict in writing for the Church because the manner in which I think about each task, or challenge, proceeds from the same starting point and can be made manifest in a variety of ways.

What does affect me in a more specific sense is the already mentioned difference between a congregation and an audience. Church attenders may like or dislike a new piece, but the purpose of their visit to the church is not, primarily, to judge or to 'get their money's worth'. This means that I have a particular responsibility when composing liturgical music. There is a congregation of people who want to be present. They haven't paid to hear my music. They have come to church to participate in an act of worship. They know the order of service and this ritual gives security, comfort, a sense of place and history, and a structure to the proceedings. As a composer, my task is not to please in any superficial sense. I am contributing to the complex mixture of which this ritual/ service consists. I have the weight of tradition behind me. Any composer writing for Christ Church Cathedral, Oxford, for example, must be aware of a great work such as the *Missa Gloria tibi Trinitas* written during his time in the 1520s at what was then Cardinal College by the Master of the Choristers, John Taverner. Style does not enter the arena in any sense, but the sense of a living tradition to be continued whets the creative appetite. Working in, and at the service of, a living environment and writing with a service order in mind is a challenge and, in the best sense, presents a problem to be solved. In the case of concert music, any piece may be put with any other for a variety of reasons, ranging from the artistic to the commercial. By comparison with, say, a great cathedral, a concert hall is an artificial environment. Some modern arts centres are, of course, lively places and a fine player will, naturally, transcend the antiseptic surroundings in which many concerts take place. The church, or cathedral, is the antithesis of this. The service is a living manifestation of a body of thought, feeling, intellectual and spiritual endeavour over centuries and writing music for use as part of it is an enormous privilege.

Two final matters emerge from this. Continuing a tradition responsibly does not mean producing what is expected in the simplest sense. The challenge is neither to aim for some kind of originality (what artist really ever thinks in that way?), nor to churn out what might be easy, but to imagine the atmosphere of the service, the choral sound, the nature of the building, and to create anew from within the tradition. Arnold Schoenberg (1874–1951) put this finely and wisely when giving young composers advice in the USA at the end of his life: 'You must learn from the Masters from whom I learned . . . but then you take the essence and create something new . . . [Y]ou must not imitate.'[6] What I am trying to say in this context could not be better put. In my pieces for liturgical use, I made no conscious attempt to make the music sound ecclesiastical (whatever that may mean), but by the same token, neither did I ignore the fact that I have known the sound of polyphonic Roman Catholic and Anglican church music all my life and love the acoustics and atmosphere of our great cathedrals. So, I began work with the task clear in my mind. Any aspects of the tradition which emerge are simply to do with prior absorption into my musical bloodstream. In other words, what you hear is the result of my usual working methods; I can soften it, or toughen it up at will, but composers have done that for centuries. In this way, I did not have to 'don a liturgical composition hat' at my desk, as I said at the beginning, writing the music as I would a concert piece, but with the advantage of knowing for what and whom I was writing, and why. This is the only time when a composer today is in the same position as, for example, Bach. The challenge is to try to create work which is alive, exactly because one is working within, and at the service of, a living tradition.

Writing liturgically, one must be as direct and as practical as possible, considering carefully matters of intonation, choral texture, rhythmic problems and other issues. As my own work usually stems from spiritual, religious and philosophical roots, the reason why I have spent time today pondering the issue of spirituality and the sacred in creative work, is that I have consciously developed working methods which enable me to move from a complex concert piece to a more obviously practical liturgical work without altering my aesthetic stance or my technique and style. I have been obsessed for many years by ideas of cycles, circles, ellipses and returns and have developed harmonic and long-range structural methods in order to write pieces which embody these concepts. The titles of some of my pieces illustrate this: I have already mentioned *Canticum Luminis*; *The Ring of Eternity*; *The Circles of Light* (a purely instrumental work based on a passage from the 'Paradiso' in Dante's *Divine Comedy*; *In the Beginning* (an orchestral piece which creates a huge circle, a paradox as music can only go in one direction and which refers both to Genesis and the music's symbolic harmonic procedures); *Songs, Dances and Ellipses* (a string quartet concerned with planet cycles combined with dance and song, the body and the voice, so basic to human worship as a means of celebration, praise and, when necessary, mourning).[7]

Music to Celebrate the Resurrection of Christ, commissioned by the BBC TV's religious department, was an interesting task.[8] I worked closely with a television producer in order to fulfil the brief and, simultaneously combined this with my 'darkness to light' train of thought. We set the ten-minute piece in

Coventry Cathedral (where, of course, Britten's *War Requiem* had received its premiere nearly thirty years earlier), the central visual images being Epstein's powerful and intentionally earth-bound 'Ecce Homo' and Graham Sutherland's tapestry of the risen Christ in majesty. The Epstein sculpture stands in the bomb-damaged ruins of the old cathedral, the Sutherland tapestry behind the altar in Basil Spence's 1960s building and they face each other in a manner that is deeply moving. I did not write music to fit the video, but told the producer what I was going to do; he then made the images to follow the music's progress from darkness, through an increasingly energetic dance towards a positive, affirmative conclusion, the face of Christ on the Sutherland tapestry filling the screen, before intense light obliterated even this. This was not conventionally liturgical in any sense, but its imagery and fundamental conception were specific in terms of Christian belief and aspirations.

So, in order to compose for liturgical purposes, I have to alter very little in my thought processes, intentions or technical methods. I have established that I do not believe that liturgical music should be either populist or trendy, but I also do not feel that a grammatical or stylistic vacuum is really alive either. If a tradition is truly strong and alive, then natural change is vital. Tallis did not compose the same music as Dunstable, and Tippett's glorious and unique *Magnificat and Nunc Dimittis*, written for St John's College, Cambridge, hard though it is to sing, continues a great tradition, but refreshes it from within. Recently, in Worcester College Chapel, I heard a Mass by my predecessor as Fellow in Music, Robert Sherlaw-Johnson; a work utterly devoid of routine, cliché or naive simplification (rather than simplicity). It sounded utterly natural and suited the service perfectly; the choir enjoyed singing it. This is encouraging. If I have a prescription for the future (and I am wary of prophecies) it is that music for the Church can be written which displays its post-Renaissance heritage and which, as composers as fine as Britten, Rubbra (one of my other predecessors at Worcester College), Tippett and, more recently, Jonathan Harvey have demonstrated, can rejuvenate from within and without a single cobweb in sight.

5

Requiem for Magnificat

ANDREW CARTER

As a young man in my twenties I was fortunate to have the dual and daily experience of singing bass in an English cathedral choir and directing the music in a Roman Catholic convent school. A third ecumenical element soon entered the equation, for I met and married a Quaker lass and became a member of the Society of Friends. For a musician it was a fascinating view. While the Catholics were merrily throwing out all things Latin, the Anglican cathedral was for the first time allowing Latin texts for the Palestrina and Byrd Masses, hitherto sung in ugly translation. Up the road at the convent I found myself scribbling settings to many new and experimental word forms. But it was tinged with a great regret that in its rush for the vernacular the Vatican had thrown out many of its musical babies with the bathwater. Conversely, down at the Protestant cathedral, evensong seemed to be set in 1662 concrete with not so much as a rustle in the rubric. In the psalms we continued to 'grin like dogs', 'went a-whoring with our own inventions' and became 'like a bottle in the smoke' to the bafflement of ourselves and the summer visitors. But while the psalms, with their vast account of the human condition, changed day by day, yet Magnificat and Nunc Dimittis processed in side by side, day in, day out, in threadbare robes and past their retirement age. Could we not sometimes have the alternative Evening Canticles, printed right there in the *Book of Common Prayer*? Almost as a Pauline conversion came my first Quaker Meeting for Worship where out of the silence there was an occasional spontaneous spoken ministry which seemed to transcend credal and musical straitjackets.

A generation later I attended evensong recently at one of our great English cathedrals, and had to confront my own ambivalence about it. Part of me is still the perpetual wide-eyed music student; part the hoary old lay-clerk cynic turned 'free church'. Here, as in many other cathedrals and colleges on our island, we have a glorious and unique heritage; something to be cherished; a unique contribution of daily musical worship over four hundred years, in the hands of consummate professionals. But here too is something remote from the people, closed off, more often than not, behind the medieval monastic choir screen and couched in medieval language by men who like to assume strange dress and funny voices – an English anachronism to go with judges' wigs and changing of the palace guard.

I was not really surprised to discover that the 'vain repetitions' of Responses and Canticles remain the same. Beautifully sung, the words retained little meaning for me. It seemed that after a century disrupted by world wars and assailed by rapid change there was a desperate clinging on to the familiar and comfortable past. But how many times can we be expected to hear or sing the Gloria suffix in one service before our linguistic senses are dulled, and with them our spiritual ones? If we need Versicles and Responses, do their petitions have to be mind-numbingly the same every day? Since many of our cathedral organists seem to regard the penning of a set of Responses as a rite of passage (as weekly BBC Radio 3 evensongs demonstrate), could we not at least hope for some dialogue between priest and musician that would produce something fresh? Or will the age-old rivalries between deans and organists for the 'spotlight', of which the recent conflict in Westminster Abbey is only the latest squalid example, prevent imaginative change and peaceful reform? In the moribund atmosphere that prevails, will things change overnight with a latter-day Dissolution of the Monasteries? Or will the creeping secularism of our British society undermine the whole crumbling edifice?

What I find true of the tiny world of English cathedrals may well be the case with other denominations. The 'nonconformist' churches, which in their own turn broke away from the rituals of the 'established' Church, soon evolved their own familiar patterns and rigid habits. In broad musical terms the effects seem strikingly different, nationally. In Germany, the grand spectacle of the Renaissance Mass made way for the grand spectacle of the Bach cantata. By contrast, after the brief flowering of Purcell and the Restoration 'verse' anthem, Protestant music in Britain aspired only to the metrical psalm and the Methodist hymn book. Each in their turn, whether in art music or folk music, attempted to breathe new life into the gospel message.

So, with the ever-quickening pace of change in our own time, when one is more likely to meet one's neighbour in the supermarket aisle than the south transept, how do I stand as a composer of church music in the new millennium? Spiritually and financially challenged, I think! Out in the real world, composers are remunerated when their works are performed in a concert hall to a paying audience – not much, but nevertheless something. In a church service, where nobody pays for entry, God gets his music for free. A budding composer of church music should come with a ready sense of vocation and private means.

Musically I have little problem, except the usual one of waiting for (divine) inspiration. When it comes I try to balance a general tunefulness with a few mild challenges for the singers and players, and out in the congregation I see in my mind's eye those who listen with an unsophisticated ear and who seek a glimpse of the eternal. Somehow one hopes that the music and the words will combine to be a bridge between the humdrum and the heavenly.

Perhaps once in a lifetime, if you are lucky, you are given the chance to write for a famous choir and a famous building. In my case I was invited to write a setting of the Latin Mass for use in the Sunday morning Eucharist at St Paul's Cathedral, London. My challenge was twofold: to write something for first-rate professionals to get their teeth into, and, for the great congregation that gathers under Wren's dome, to translate into musical terms the thought so well expressed in: 'This is none other than the house of God, and this is the gate of heaven' (Genesis 28.17). Somehow, at one and the same time I had to reach into my own spiritual depths while consciously remembering that ordinary folk are out there listening – the likes of my Mum and your sister whose daily diet might be the musak of local radio. In the hosannas of the Sanctus, therefore, helped by the rolling acoustic of that vast space, and after the example of illustrious precedents, I tried to paint a vision of the eternal city in the antiphonal shouts of the eight-part choir, punctuated by dramatic chords from the enormous organ. By contrast, where the Agnus Dei lays emphasis on our human vulnerability at the central point of the communion, a simple and direct melody, floating on the boys' voices, gives gentle balm to our flawed condition.

Back in evensong, my mind wandered off, and I imagined God himself conducting interviews for the post of Composer of Heavenly Music. Handel was a strong contender, but poor old Bach wasn't even called. Purcell was in with a chance. Stanford managed the short list for his spinning-wheel *Magnificat in* G. Herbert Howells got short shrift: 'Have you ever written a tune?' and 'Are you the one who writes Magnificats ad nauseam?' Verdi, Puccini and Sondheim were each in for twenty minutes. Britten was soon on his way out looking stony faced. Fauré was on the telephone enquiring if his application had been received. Finally it was between

Monteverdi and Andrew Lloyd Webber. 'Ah, Mr Lloyd Webber, I like your *Pie Jesu*. When can you start?'

For the earthbound composer finding a suitable text often proves to be the most difficult starting point. The words must leap off the page at you, inspiring you to your creative best. They must have their own poetry and beauty, which is why many of us still find the Authorized Version of the Bible beguiling. Given the pedestrian language in much of modern liturgy, who can blame us? There is, however, still a rich store of beautiful sacred verse and prose from our own times and earlier that remains untapped. As composers we should go out and look for it rather than reaching habitually for the Psalms or the Early English carol texts. Many familiar verses have been done to death by musicians who lacked the time or imagination to read more widely. And it is a brave or fool-hardy writer who ventures to set new music to well-known double acts like the words of 'Hark, the herald angels sing' and the music of Mendelssohn, to take an uncontroversial example. To do so is to invite comparison. Better, surely, to bequeath a 'new' text to the listeners. We must also be sensi-tive to questions of gender and inclusive language. 'Dear Lord and father of mankind' is just as much yesterday's speech for some as thees, thous and thereuntos.

Clearly the music itself must be melodious, as Handel was quick to spot, and must let the words speak out fresh to both performers and listeners, and perhaps to God too. 'Nothing,' said the Council of Trent in 1562, 'is to interfere with the easy intelligibility of the text'. God himself will take in his stride the intricacies of Tallis's forty-part counterpoint along with the astringencies of Tippett's *St John's Service*, or more lately James MacMillan's angular and uncompromising carol com-mission for King's College, Cambridge. This is music of the professionals for the professionals and will appeal to a small constituency of discriminating perception. But what about the rest of us here on humble earth?

Implicit in my understanding of music in worship is the idea that 'God loveth a cheerful giver' (2 Corinthians 9.7). Today, the spectacle of a large crowd singing rousing mission hymns on a holiday beach must tell us something. A century or so ago the Revivalist movement brought with it that same evangelical awareness that a simple and catchy tune would help draw the crowds. Even as late as 1950, I took it for granted as a ten-year-old in our family handbell group, that 'Count your blessings' (No. 745 in Sankey's *Sacred Songs and Solos*) would be a favourite request when we paid our annual visit to the local pub. Everybody knew it and joined in lustily. It was the same sort of response to a lively tune that I noticed in the nearby Methodist chapel, a spontaneous joy in the song and the singing of it that was painfully absent in my own Anglican parish church at the top of the same street. I noticed too that it was similar in style to the music-hall ballads mother sang around the house.

Quick to surface in such musings is the question of taste! How do we as composers assume the common touch without being commonplace or even 'common'? How can we give the best of our artistic selves in the service of God and at the same time appeal with our integrity intact to 'ordinary folk'? The questions themselves are not new, so perhaps the answers don't have to be new either. Mozart in his *Eine Kleine* mode managed some successful Mass settings. Bach's *Jesu joy* continues to weave its spell. There is no reason at all why our own tunesmithing for the Church should not be just as enticing, save perhaps for our own ingrained snobbery, or a mistaken notion that the divine is ever severe and the devil is in the dance.

We need to be neither over-sophisticated nor over-serious in our songs of praise. And perhaps we need to see more often through the eyes of children. This was brought home to me recently in an unexpected way. My 'Badgers and Hedgehogs' is a rollicking little number written a decade ago for eight- to ten-year olds in a larger work involving adults, called *Benedicite*.[1] The children have fun in reciting a long string of alliterative animal names, invariably ending each verse with 'and badgers and hedgehogs Bless the Lord'. A friend in New York state reports that the adults in his Episcopal church choir sang it as the Sunday morning unison anthem to general approval. How long before it makes cathedral even-song?

To describe oneself as a church composer in the Britain of today is to admit to being largely unemployed. There is a spectacular lack of artistic vision across the denominational board. This is unsurprising in the Nonconformist churches that from the first relied on homespun and voluntary talent. Much the same might be said of the modern Roman Catholics in Britain. In a country that has traditionally cherished all things amateur, there is a natural suspicion of 'experts' and 'professionals'. Anyway, why pay a musician when the roof needs fixing?

For whatever reason, a general long-term decline in churchgoing is now accelerating dramatically. The knock-on effect is that the traditional parish choirs dwindle as families head for the coast (or the shopping mall). In the local parishes organists are increasingly likely to be laid off by trendy vicars, priests and ministers in favour of amplified pop groups who loudly peddle second-rate lyrics to a dumbed-down 'contemporary' style. The old guard departs. In the cathedrals, deans and provosts, saddled with enormous running costs and upkeep of historic buildings, put patronage of Saint Cecilia fairly low in their priorities. Other than the occasional centenary, enthronement of a bishop or monarch's coronation (last one 1953), composers can expect to look elsewhere.

That 'elsewhere' in my case is either the concert hall, where British choral societies perform one or other of my longer sacred or secular works, or in the much more vibrantly alive religious atmosphere of America. There, by comparison, I find a great freshness of spirit, a get-up-and-go feeling that encourages creativity. I have fulfilled a variety of commissions for Presbyterian, Methodist and Lutheran churches, and a Quaker college. In many average middle-sized towns, it seems, each denomination supports a full-time, fully trained church musician who runs, typically, an adult choir; one or two children's choirs; a youth choir; adult and junior handbell groups. In the larger towns he or she is certainly likely to have a full- or part-time assistant. The 'Let's do it' factor is evident in high standards of performance. You can expect excellent organ accompaniments and solos. To find the roots of this tradition one looks to continental Europe and in particular to Lutheran Germany.

In a nation well known for its love of celebrating, the American churches frequently add colour to their services by using in-house instrumentalists, or for special occasions hiring in an orchestra to accompany a cantata or a new commission. Of my American premieres written for chorus and orchestra, all have been accompanied by instrumentalists of outstanding ability. An extra bonus for an Englishman is that they seem to enjoy playing too. At home in Britain we could learn much from our American colleagues.

Much as I personally love writing for the organ, I appreciate that in the wrong hands (and, if you're unlucky, feet) it is hardly an aid to Christian thought. My great aunt Aggie, who was already old when I was in my enquiring teens, spoke fondly about the time when singing in our church was accompanied by a band of instruments in the west gallery – fiddles, bassoons and the like. Soon, to her regret, the gallery was swept away, and the players replaced by the 'one man band' in the chancel. Aunt Aggie must have had a say in a memorable Californian commission I accepted in the early 1990s. It began as a simple request for a five-minute anthem for choir and organ to celebrate the opening of a lovely new church. Honoured, I set to work. But as the weeks

progressed, I received a constant flow of afterthoughts by fax
or telephone from the director of music, Gary Purvis:

Brr, brr:
'I'm thinking of adding a few wind instruments – flute,
oboe, clarinet, bassoon, horn?'
'Fine.'
Brr, brr:
'The bassoonist's wife is also a very good bassoonist. Two
bassoons?'
'Yep. O.K.'
Brr, brr:
'We should include the junior choir – fairly young –
nothing above upper D?' 'Sure.'
Brr, brr:
'The ladies of the handbell team. . . .'
'Yes, all right.'
Brr, brr, scroll, scroll:
'I have a nice baritone soloist. Is there a line or two . . . ?'
'I'll try.'
Brr, brr:
'I'd forgotten to mention our lovely harp player, started a
year ago.'
'No promises.'
Brr, brr:
'Gary here . . .'
'Don't tell me, let me guess. Soprano solo?'
'Yes please!'
'Well, as long as this is the last thing, time's running short.'
Brr, brr, scroll, scroll:
'Dear Andrew, thanks for the vocal score. It's a fantastic
piece. I was thinking that it just needs a final hymn for the
congregation to join in. Can you write the words as well?'
'_____ _____!'
Brr, brr:

'It's Gary'

'Now, Gary, before you start, the answer is no. I'm busy sorting the orchestral parts out.'

'I just wanted to tell you that we practised the hymn with the congregation on Sunday morning. It's terrific. We're absolutely thrilled. The sopranos wondered if there's a teeny-weeny chance of a soaring descant?'

I flew over for the opening of the new church a few days later and to a very successful premiere of my new fifteen-minute cantata, *Great is the Lord* – on time and under budget. It remains unpublished.

6

Beyond a Mass for Westminster

ROXANNA PANUFNIK

[*This chapter is based on Roxanna Panufnik's conversation with Stephen Darlington and Christopher Rowland, Dean Ireland's Professor of the Exegesis of Holy Scripture, Oxford University.*]

SD It was a great honour when you were asked to write the *Westminster Mass*, which I believe was commissioned to celebrate the late Cardinal Basil Hume's seventy-fifth birthday.[1] How did it happen that you were asked to write this piece?
RP The Mass was commissioned by the John Studzinski Foundation for young artists, which is run by a very close personal friend of the late Cardinal. This friend was stuck for an idea of what to give the Cardinal for his birthday because the Cardinal hated any kind of fuss or attention. He didn't want a party and he didn't want any big material gifts. So this friend struck on the idea of commissioning a piece of music, because the Cardinal's two main loves in life were the music of Westminster Cathedral and his projects to help the homeless. Then the search started for a composer. The Cardinal was very keen on supporting 'youth' and I was still in my twenties then. It was also known that I was a practising Catholic – not a very devout one, but practising nevertheless. So I was approached and asked to send tapes of my music to the Foundation and to the Cathedral to make sure that my style of music would be suitable for what the Cathedral choir was used to singing. Once that was approved and I was hired, there came a period of very close collaboration with the

Cathedral to determine what exactly they wanted from a Mass. For instance, they didn't want a Credo because it is very rare to have a sung Credo now, and there are certain precise lengths for each part of the Mass. For example, during the Agnus Dei, the priest is standing there with his arms up in the air, so if it is too long then he is going to get very tired. I did in fact overshoot the mark by about 40 seconds and there were terrible complaints afterwards!

My other specific instruction was that the Cardinal wanted the Mass to be in English, in his words 'to enhance the liturgy for the new millennium'. So my task was to write a work that really emphasized and dramatized – it was a great word-painting exercise – the words of the Mass. And they are very dramatic; there is something very theatrical about the Catholic Mass and the ritual that comes with it. The smells and the priests and the way the whole service is conducted have a great air of theatre about them. So that was my task. I became a practising Catholic late in life, when I was 21. I had a pretty agnostic upbringing and because I became a Catholic relatively late I had missed out on all the Sunday school and instruction through childhood that young Catholics normally get. So when, at age 29, I was commissioned to do this Mass, I had to get a lot of extra theological instruction and a lot of extra help. Every Sunday in Mass when I was saying the words of the Kyrie and the Gloria and the Sanctus and Benedictus, I never really understood, word for word, what they meant. It became a very automatic thing. Once you learn those words off by heart you just say them, and it can be part of the very comforting meditative ritual of going to Mass. So I had a couple of months of going through the words of the Mass with a fine toothcomb, guided by a priest, Fr Vladimir Felzmann. I also asked Cardinal Hume where I could go on retreat – some place where I could get away from the confusions and distractions of life, the telephone and everything else, and where there would be really good music. He recommended Stanbrook Abbey in Worcestershire, an enclosed order of 34 Benedictine nuns, who do the most fantastic singing of plainsong. Their sound is really magical. I ended up spending a lot of time at this abbey at the foot of the Malvern Hills. It was the perfect setting and I became great friends with the nuns there, particularly Sister Margaret who is the organist and Sister Rafael who is extremely knowledgeable about the liturgy and who was responsible for a lot of my inspiration. If ever I was stuck I would just talk to her for five minutes and her brightness and her enthusiasm would whip up the muse immediately. So that was the start of a ten-month process. It was a long process, the composition of the Mass.

SD You said that you were asked to send some examples of your compositions. How much of that music was specifically sacred?

RP Very little, in fact, none at all. I had written very little sacred music as such. There was a string quartet and there was, funnily enough, an environmental cantata that I was commissioned to write at the height of the environmental enthusiasm in the late 1980s and early 1990s. There were some songs, but none of the examples were actually religious.

SD So do you think that they chose you because they somehow identified a spiritual element that was present in your musical language? Or was it simply that they liked the music? Is there a spiritual dimension to your composition?

RP That is something that is very hard for me to be objective about. I am told that there is, and that my music is highly emotional. The Polish side of me I think comes out very strongly in this. Also the string quartet I sent them was based on a passage from *Twelfth Night* – 'Make me a willow cabin at your gate'. This was a very literal word-painting exercise, but with no words actually involved in the piece. From this they probably felt that I had a good understanding of words. Also I think they were quite worried that they might be getting something too 'modern'. I say 'modern' in inverted commas because everybody's view of modern is different, but maybe something that might be unreachable and inaccessible to a church-going congregation who might not necessarily be musically literate or into the more challenging styles of music that we have today. There is a growing trend that is called the 'happy clappy' style of music – a sort of evangelistic kind of music – and I think they were anxious not to have that either. They wanted to have the kind of music that the congregation could engage with.

SD What are your musical roots? We were just discussing whether your musical language has an essentially spiritual dimension and you mentioned your Polish background, which you obviously feel is part of it. Could you tell us more about what sorts of ingredients combine to make your musical style?

RP Again this is a really hard thing to be objective about. I always find when people ask me to describe my own musical style it is like someone asking you to describe what you look like. But let me try. My main love, and always the point where I start my composition, is harmony. I have a great, great love of harmony, and a lot of this comes from the fact that, especially during my teenage years, I was playing the flute and the harp and I played a lot of late French Romantic music. And also my father Sir Andrzej Panufnik was, as you know, a composer. I had a lot of his music around as a child and there were very strong Polish roots in that. I was always very interested in Polish folk music as well and I used that quite a bit in my work. So, yes, it is the harmony that dominates everything that I do.

SD You mentioned to me earlier that hearing a piece by John Tavener was an inspiration for you before writing the Mass. Would that relate to what you have just said?

RP Yes, the piece was Tavener's *Hymn to the Mother of God*, which I heard at the Christmas celebration at Westminster

Cathedral just before I started work on the Mass. It was absolutely magical. All the lights had been turned off and there were hundreds of candles. Everything went very quiet. Then from the Lady Chapel, right at the very end of the cathedral, came the amazing sound of this music. Those of you who have been to Westminster Cathedral will know that there is a phenomenal delay in sound there. It is a huge place, a very high place, and I think they actually have an eight-second delay on the music, so it literally washes over you. I had already been warned by James O'Donnell, who was the Master of Music there at the time, not to make my music too complex in a contrapuntal or rhythmic way because it would be completely lost in a blur. So when I heard this piece of Tavener and the way he uses the harmonies so that they wash over each other and the way the church acoustic makes them overlap each other even more – it just knocked me for six! I thought, here are elements that help elicit the meditative and mystical aspect of worship. And I sensed, since my music is actually quite bi-tonal anyway in style, 'Right, this is the kind of thing that I am going to do.'

CR Can I go on from that Tavener piece? I think the thing that I found most striking when I listened to the *Westminster Mass* was how different your music is from Tavener's music. I think particularly of the Sanctus and the climax of the Benedictus in the *Westminster Mass*. There is a rhythmic urgency, which is often lacking in a lot of contemporary choral music of a sacred kind – music that tends to be of the reflective kind you find in Tavener, Pärt and others. Your *Westminster Mass* is very different.

RP Let me answer that by telling you a little bit of how I composed the Sanctus and Benedictus from my Mass. There is such obvious word painting it is almost embarrassing. It is so obvious, but 'Holy, Holy, Holy, Lord, God of power and might' has a big punch on 'might'. 'Heaven and earth are full of your glory' – the heaven and earth are a sort of unison which comes to a big full chord for 'full'. 'Hosanna' – it is a real celebration – expresses my mental picture of people dancing. I also had the boys of Westminster Cathedral in my head when I was writing it; they are boyish and full of enthusiasm. When it comes to the Benedictus, it is quite quiet and subdued, and then suddenly, bam, 'Hosanna' comes back again and it finishes with the beginning of the Kyrie. When I was finishing composing the Kyrie at Stanbrook Abbey, sitting in the Presbytery at the piano there, the bell started ringing for offices. So I have got the Stanbrook Abbey bell ringing at the end of both the Sanctus and Benedictus and the Kyrie.

CR I have enjoyed listening to these things over recent weeks and I think they have helped me to express things about my faith. But I wonder whether in addition to helping us see about the word-painting that has gone on, you could say what the music expressed about your Christian faith? Is it possible for you to say?

RP I think it expresses the very positive aspects of my faith. My faith came to me literally weeks before I discovered that my father had cancer. It was as if it had been put there as a safety net, and it gave me strength to survive his illness and death, and also another awful thing that happened. The reason that I became a Catholic was that I was sent to a Catholic church to find hymns for a friend's wedding – it was a research mission. I didn't find any hymns, but I found my faith. The awful thing was that during the time my father was ill, months after my friend got married, my friend committed suicide. This was completely unforeseen. It was just the most calamitous horrific time. But every Sunday when I came out of Mass I felt an amazing sense of peace and calm and a sense that I could cope with whatever was going to be thrown at me. And I felt a huge physical warmth, a great comfort and a great love, a glow inside me from Mass. I also wanted to celebrate the fact that I had been lucky enough to have this, because it doesn't come to everybody and I wasn't looking for it; it found me just at a time when I was really going to need it. So all of that – all the broken heart, and all the survival and the strength that I gained from having been through that – is in the *Westminster Mass*, which was an opportunity for me publicly to celebrate how I felt, because I am not very good at explaining how I feel in words. It was really huge for me. And in fact something amazing happened when I was writing the Kyrie. I was at Stanbrook Abbey, working on this progression of sort of repentant harmonies for the Kyrie. I was sitting at the piano and there was nobody else around. Suddenly I heard my father's voice very clearly – he had been dead for six years – saying, 'Roxanna, clean up your. harmonies.' Which, of course, I didn't. I had never listened to him when he was alive, so I wasn't going to listen to him now! But it shows how the Mass was a coming home for me. It was a summation of everything that I had been through over those last six years. It was a great emotional journey, a fabulous therapy.

CR One of the things that comes across to me particularly in the climax to the Sanctus and Benedictus is the cosmopolitan nature that seems to be expressed in your music. I wonder whether you wanted to write music for men and women who are Catholic, for men and women who are going to Mass Sunday by Sunday, to help them in their worship of God.

RP This is a tricky thing, partly because a huge part of the congregation in most Catholic churches is quite transient. In order to teach a congregation new music that they are going to sing every week, there has to be a really strong regular body of people who are going to be there in order to do that. And also, when do you teach them? I remember saying to somebody, 'Oh, well you start them all off ten minutes before Mass every Sunday. You could work on a little bit before that.' And that person said. 'But that ten minutes before Mass is when you arrive and when you say your own personal prayers and you put yourself in the frame of mind that you want to be in during Mass.'

This brings in the question of how much would congregations and audiences *like* to participate in the music of the service? Indeed, what is participation, because participation does not necessarily have to be singing and actually making the music? Participation can be listening. When a congregation is listening to a reading it does not mean that they are not participating in the Mass any more. This is a difficult thing, and I have yet to form my own ideas of balance between how much congregations want to participate and how much they want to be sung to. In preparation for today I asked my priest at my local church in Chiswick if I could circulate a survey among the congregation about their feelings about music in worship, and he said, 'Oh, no, no, no, no, please don't do that because the Latinists will come out and start complaining again.' This signified to me that there is a core of people who very much enjoy having the plainsong and the traditional elements of the service, and now there is a lot of what they call 'folk services' in worship. The feeling I have when I go to these 'folk' Masses is that the congregation around me are quite reluctant; it is as though they are being forced to syncopate. It is a difficult question, and there should be more research into what congregations want. I wish there would be, but obviously people are reluctant to stir up any strong feelings about what was and isn't happening at the moment.

CR If your parish in Chiswick came along and said, 'Roxanna, would you compose a congregational Mass for us,' would you be keen to do it?

RP Oh yes, but I'd spend a lot of time talking to the congregation about what they would and wouldn't want. I'd listen a lot to them first before I tried to do something like that.

CR Can I ask a final question and change gear entirely? Can you reflect with us on what it is like being a woman who is composing in a male world, the male world of church music which applies just as much to Westminster Cathedral as it does to the Church of England? And also, could you reflect on why there have been so few women composers down the centuries?

RP I was about to say that I don't particularly notice that I am a woman, but I think that would be lying! It doesn't seem to be an issue when I am working. But you are right. You could count the number of female composers on the fingers of one hand who are currently at the forefront of British music. And I am often asked why.

I think it is one of those jobs which women don't particularly think of doing. There are very few role models. Lots of women study composition at both university and college, but as soon as they leave there is a dramatic drop-off rate. My theory is that, whatever the feminists say, women and men are very different. When it comes to thinking about the long-term future, women tend to be more pragmatic – being a composer isn't a very sensible thing to do.

It wasn't easy for me. I left music college swearing never to write another note again, because I wasn't getting good marks. It was during the mid-1980s when esoteric and cerebral avant-garde music was still considered the right kind of music to be writing. My professors, rightly in some ways, were encouraging me to be a bit more experimental. But I just didn't want to. I felt very false and that I wasn't being true to myself in writing that kind of music, so I didn't. And my end of college graduation report said, 'Roxanna has a great gift for melody but her music is naïve.' I kind of thought, 'Well, maybe I'm not a good composer after all and I'll go and do something else.' So I went to the BBC for two years to work in television as a researcher. But my contemporaries at music college, while I was working at the BBC, were still performing my work and asking me for pieces. So I began to build up some self-confidence again. But it was the death of my father and an amazing conversation I had with him just before he died that made me think, 'You know, life is too short not to be doing what you really want to do. I want to compose. And I have no responsibilities – no children and no huge mortgage – so I'm going to do it!' And also I felt: if I can survive that bereavement then I can do anything. And so I did it. I had to be very one-track minded about it. When you are working and composing, you have to be able to completely shut everything else off. Every morning for three hours I turn the telephone bells off, the answerphone is on and I shut my door and the outside world is completely gone. Women are incredibly good at thinking about more than one thing at a time, and I think it's very hard to discipline yourself and to be really one-track minded. And of course there is the thing of when children come along it is just almost impossible to cut yourself off from that instinctive bind. It wasn't really an issue when I was writing the Mass. I never thought, 'Hey, I'm working with all these men, and they are all boys' voices.' Although someone did tell me that somebody in the orchestra made the ambiguous comment, 'Oh, you can tell a woman wrote this.' Whether it meant that I wear my heart on my sleeve, I don't know. That is not to say that men don't wear their hearts on their sleeves, but perhaps women are more obvious about it.

SD Are you optimistic about the future of music in the Church?

RP Yes, yes. The market for church music in the record industry – particularly in the last four or five years – has been phenomenal. And it is not just the church-going public who are buying CDs of Tavener and Pärt and plainsong and the monks of Ampleforth and Hildegard von Bingen in their millions. I am hugely optimistic, because I think people, having lived through the materialistic 1980s and the caring 1990s, are now looking for another dimension, a spiritual dimension. They are wanting to be moved. I am very optimistic about the future of religious music.

7

Worship in Spirit and in Truth

GRAHAM KENDRICK

When the Samaritan woman at Jacob's well posed a question about worship to the Jewish stranger, the apparent simplicity of her words belied the multitude of divisive issues lurking behind them, not least centuries of religious and racial prejudice. She could well have expected an answer which unpacked the past. Instead Jesus' response dealt with the future and the present: 'A time is coming and has now come.' Jesus declared,

> Believe me, woman, a time is coming when you will worship the Father neither on this mountain nor in Jerusalem . . . A time is coming and has now come when the true worshippers will worship the Father in spirit and truth, for they are the kind of worshippers that the Father seeks. God is spirit, and his worshippers must worship in spirit and in truth. (John 4.21–24 NIV)

In the midst of our contemporary debates about how we should – or would like to – worship, often the last question we consider is what God may be looking for. That is where we all should start. Similarly, those who seek to compose music for Christian worship should have as their first priority to be the kind of worshipper the Father seeks.

But there is something in this passage that is often missed. Here we have Jesus' most comprehensive teaching about worship. But to whom is he speaking? Who is getting not only an exclusive seminar but also a frank declaration of his messiahship?

Jesus' congregation at the well side was not his 'church' of disciples but a lost sinner. Probably a social pariah in her own village (she came to the well alone), as a Samaritan a racial pariah as far as the Jews were concerned, she had a confused theology, a convoluted ancestry, a despised gender and a suspect morality. But Jesus was the one who always saw and did what the Father was doing, and here he saw a woman whom the Father was seeking to be a true worshipper.

Any discussion about the future of worship music would do well to take place against the background of this incident and its poignant reminder that the Father's call to become true worshippers is to a world of sinners. It is not to an exclusive worship 'club' of believers shut away behind walls.

The origins and development of contemporary praise and worship

My task in this chapter is to focus on composing music for Christian worship in the category popularly known as 'contemporary praise and worship'. It is important to point out that this is not an exclusive category. In some churches today such songs are commonly used alongside other more traditional forms of church music, though in many churches this category would predominate.

In order to see where we may be going, it is often helpful to see where we have come from. What has caused this kind of song to spread throughout an ever-widening swathe of English Christianity?

'Indeed the water I give him will become in him a spring of water welling up to eternal life' (John 4.14). The source of the current wave of contemporary praise and worship songs can be traced back to the 'well' from which the charismatic and Pentecostal movements have drunk. At a time when much traditional Christianity has experienced decline, these movements have had enormous influence worldwide, and have cherished emphases which have been very fruitful, not only in stimulating new music, but also in emphasizing the priority of worship itself.

What emphases have been characteristic of the movements from which the new music has come? One emphasis is the recovery of the 'priesthood of all believers' as opposed to a church dominated by professional clergy; this has released many gifts, which may otherwise have been marginalized. A second emphasis is a fervent commitment to evangelism and mission; this has not only encouraged the building of cultural bridges towards the world at large but has replenished congregations with previously unchurched people, many of whom were never exposed to traditional forms of Christian worship in the first place. A third emphasis, a high regard for the scriptures, has given rise to the practice of singing literal scriptures or close paraphrases put to music. A fourth emphasis, fellowship, has brought about a proliferation of home groups. In these, simple worship is accompanied by acoustic instruments; the songs have to be simple, instant and accessible on a 'folk' level. Fifth, an emphasis on baptism in the Holy Spirit and the gifts of the Spirit has encouraged the development of a worship culture which is both spontaneous and participative, and where many songs are birthed spontaneously.

Stylistically, these new movements have been more willing than traditional churches to draw on popular music culture, so that the contemporary praise and worship songs that originate in them have sometimes been light-heartedly dubbed 'baptized rock and roll'. The domination of the three-and-a-half minute radio pop song in popular culture has largely shaped the genre of the worship chorus – rhythmic, instant, strong on emotion, light in content. The presentation of these songs is also loosely modelled on the singer and his or her band. The phenomenon has followed the massive cultural and social changes begun in the 1960s and has flourished in a climate of social change, eclecticism, innovation and flexibility. This is a culture both of a desire for spiritual experience and, to a degree, of disposability. Its music has become the 'establishment sound' of much of the baby-boomer generation, and now their children are repeating the process in the terms of their own cultures, tastes and styles.

As weeknight home groups have become a common feature of the life of many churches, praise music and worship has passed into the hands of whoever strums the most chords – and simple accessible songs have proved most practical. These songs have flourished with the help of new technologies, such as the overhead projector, which has not only made it easier to use songs too new for the hymn book but has also facilitated spontaneity and flexibility in the act of worship. Now the Internet and computer technology are making the currency of songs simple to spread and exchange on a global scale.

In the 1980s and 1990s Bible weeks, festivals and conferences of many kinds flourished, spawning popular worship leaders, stimulating songwriting and generating a cross-denominational audience. From its genesis at the end of the 1970s, the cross-denominational Spring Harvest teaching and worship event became an annual stimulus for songs on the year's chosen theme. My own song, 'The servant king', derived its title from the theme for 1983. New publishing companies were formed to serve the new movements, producing a growing stream of songbooks, recordings and worship resources.

These songs have spread as people have accepted that they can be incorporated into the worship of a variety of traditions. And, of course, a large proportion of the people converted into the new churches have no background in any Christian worship tradition whatever, no residual knowledge of hymns or liturgical texts.

My own journey as a worship leader and writer of praise

and worship songs has been in the context of these changes and developments. I grew up in a music-loving household, one of four children of a Baptist pastor, harmonizing by ear around the piano after church. When a frustrated piano teacher gave up on me – I insisted on learning the exercises by ear and pretending to read the notes when I couldn't! – I took a dislike to formal music education. Later, when I took an interest in the guitar, I determined to teach myself to play by ear. I became part of a band playing in evangelistic coffee bars, and I wrote most of the songs that we sang. I developed into the singer-songwriter role during my time in teacher training college and, after a post-graduation gap year travelling the country doing concerts, I found opportunities opening up in recording, performance, worship-leading and songwriting.

During a summer vacation from college I had experienced the baptism in the Holy Spirit and discovered a dimension of worship I had not previously known. This also exposed me to the first wave of simple worship songs, which, by the way, I regarded as simplistic and slightly embarrassing. Yet I had to recognize that in the meetings where they were sung something was going on that I could not deny: the presence of God came, and people poured out their hearts with an enthusiasm and feeling I had not previously known. When I complained one day to a friend, Clive Calver, he challenged me: 'You're a songwriter – you write some choruses you *do* like.' The first batch of these sprang out of the worship times and relationships of the small team that Clive and I were working with at the time, and lay unpublished for several years while I continued performing my singer/songwriter role in colleges, schools and concert venues. I was called on more and more to lead extempore praise and worship, and demand for the new songs grew as the various renewal movements steadily became mainstream.

Stylistically, the soft rock style predominated at first but, more recently, a welcome diversification of style has taken place, making room for eclectic influences: dance, Celtic, chant, black gospel, urban gospel, soul. At the same time, there has been an increase in the use of computer visuals, video and sound samples as the worship experience has come to involve our many senses. To accommodate a widening variety of worship tastes, many churches now offer 'multiple choice worship', from prayer book communion services to family services, even to 'raves in the nave'.

Postmodern thought patterns have encouraged an emphasis on the subjective experience of the worshipper, leading to a new wave of first personal pronoun songs which reflect and stimulate experience, rather than declaring objective truth.

The subject matter of praise and worship songs often reflects popular theological trends within the movements that spawn them, for example, the Vineyard Movement's emphasis on intimacy with God through worship. Other movements emphasize victory, celebration or faith confessions. There has also been a welcome rediscovery or repackaging of some traditional hymns, especially those suitable for arrangement in a broadly Celtic style, which reflects people's search for roots and certainties in the past rather than the present. I also believe that this is partly motivated by a hunger for a richer theological content – and a deeper mystical content – which many people feel that the choruses lack.

Publishing contemporary praise and worship songs, which really only got under way in the 1980s, has become very influential, and new songs, recordings, songbooks and computer resources proliferate. In many churches, platform performance – assisted by related technology from public address systems to digital projection – has displaced pulpit-centred services. The microphone has profoundly affected church worship culture. 'Personality' worship leaders and songwriters have arisen and become figureheads, and the influence of churches or movements that have pioneered a new sound or style goes round the world at an unprecedented speed. Some worship bands have set their sights on invading popular culture with music that carries the spirit and motive of worship but with a more subtle content designed to relate to the non-believer searching for spiritual answers to their felt needs.

The content of true worship

If one is to compose music for Christian worship it is vital to understand what constitutes true Christian worship. My own understanding in its simplest form is based upon the words of Jesus that we have already considered from John chapter 4. These can be summed up under three headings:

(a) *Worship the Father*: true worship is not the music itself. But music is a God-given means through which we can express the overflow of our personal relationship with God. Such a relationship comes as a consequence of faith in Christ, resulting in spiritual regeneration. Simply put, a worship service with the God we love is more than the music, just as a meal with someone we love is more than the food.

(b) *In spirit*: true worship is a function of the regenerated spirit, and is facilitated and enlightened by the Holy Spirit.

(c) *In truth*: true worship is based on the actual historical events of God's 'salvation story' recorded in the scriptures. Its content is the revelation of Christ through the teachings of the apostles and prophets. It requires sincerity, 'truth in the inward parts' (Psalm 51.6), and integrity – the whole of life is an offering to God.

True Christian worship is not merely an individual activity. On the contrary, because God is a fellowship of Father, Son and Holy Spirit, the worship that most glorifies God is that which flows from the fellowship of believers as they seek to love one another.

Praise and worship songs, their content and the ways in

which they are used have been strongly influenced by certain understandings among charismatic Christians of what worship is. Here is a sample of these:

(a) Worship involves the whole person: body, mind and spirit – therefore it is about participation not observation. Music can engage the whole person, whether by active participation or by listening.

(b) God is present as we worship through the Holy Spirit, and as we come to him, he comes to us, and may manifest his presence. The participants generally have the expectation that the Holy Spirit will direct the worship, often through the operation of the gifts of prophecy, tongues and the other revelatory gifts. Music, especially when sensitively and skilfully used, can shape the ebb and flow of worship, and can change direction in response to God's presence.

(c) Worship is both vertical and horizontal. Prayer and prophesying are both offerings to God and gifts from God, and they are open for all to participate in (1 Corinthians 14.26). Music can facilitate 'speaking to one another with psalms, hymns and spiritual songs' (Ephesians 5.19), as well as our 'conversation' with God.

(d) Worship is an overflowing of 'body life'. It comes out of a community in which daily lives are lived as unto the Lord in loving relationships; it is a product of a community of the Spirit. In the Greek New Testament, the admonition 'Be filled with Spirit' (Ephesians 5.18) is in the plural, directed to the congregation, and not in the singular, directed to individual believers. Music can unify us into common thought and common emotion. In the context of a music team as well as of a congregation, 'body-life' can be practised.

(e) Worship should be seen as a way of life and not as an activity restricted to special services and meetings, or only expressed through words and music. In the concluding section of his eucharistic liturgy, the early church father Hippolytus added this admonition, designed to ring in the ears of the worshippers as they dispersed: 'When these things have been done, each one shall hasten to do good works and to please God and to conduct himself rightly, being zealous for the Church, doing what he has learnt and advancing in piety.'[1] In other words, we must act on what we have enacted. As the writer of the letter to the Hebrews said, '[Do] not forget to do good and to share with others, for with such sacrifices God is pleased' (Hebrews 13.16). Musical expressions of worship are not a substitute for a lifestyle of worship.

(f) The Christian life is a battle. In a very real sense, it is a battle for worship, in which the world, the flesh and the devil war against the Church. We fight to call all people to worship Christ as Prince of peace, King of kings and Lord of lords, and to forsake all other gods, in particular the 'god of this world' who seeks to usurp the worship due to the creator. Music wedded to appropriate lyrics can capture the substance and spirit of vital truths, and appropriate music can help us to 'sing' these truths into our daily lives, thereby sustaining and equipping us in the battle.

(g) The culmination of worship will come when all peoples and everything created in heaven and earth will bow the knee to Christ, and the whole universe will be brought under his headship. In other words, the destiny of the universe is to worship Christ forever. Every time we sing and make music to God we anticipate the worship of heaven.

Contemporary praise and worship songs have contributed much to the changing worship of the churches. Their 'home-grown' and participatory nature brings a strong sense of belonging and identity within 'streams' and movements. They are often in the vernacular, which has popular appeal, though this also means that they can date quickly and become anachronistic.

Because these songs can travel fast and transcend 'tribal' boundaries, they can popularize current emphases such as intimacy, prayer and mission. They can also facilitate a cross-pollination of ideas between otherwise insular Christian communities. In the case of the most popular songs, they can be a common reference point and bond between different streams.

Some would argue that praise and worship songs have made church culture more accessible to unchurched people. This depends, because for those who look to church traditions for stability in a rapidly changing world, change can be negative, and they can regard the introduction of elements of contemporary music style as a trivializing factor. But the use of music, which is both accessible and requires multiple instruments, has released much latent talent in congregations where previously one person would have served alone in accompanying the singing.

Concerns in writing music for worship

What are my concerns as I write for worship? First of all, I am concerned to be sincere and genuine. Even though I may be approached to write on a given theme, I must still seek the experience that the writer of Psalm 45 had when he was able to say, 'My heart is stirred by a noble theme.' Several years ago I was asked to write a song based on the letter to the Philippians. I read and reread the letter until a phrase stirred and moved me, which, in this case, concerned Paul's passion to know Jesus. My 'Knowing you' song grew from that moment of response in my own heart as I sought to share Paul's longing.

Another concern is for the theological content. Someone once said, 'Sing me your songs and I'll tell you your theology.' There is no doubt in my mind that today a great deal of the theology we receive is through song lyrics, and it is the nearest most Christians come to scripture memorization. Hence the songwriter who may not have had even a basic theological training is in a very influential position.

Several years ago when I was in the process of recording a new album that included the song 'Meekness and majesty', I showed the lyric to a friend of mine who had been theologically trained. I will never forget how he pointed with some concern to a line in that original version described the incarnation of Christ in terms of 'clothed with humanity'. While I had thought this was a great way to describe God made flesh, he pointed out that clothes are put on and taken off whereas Christ was made flesh and remains in the form of a man in his resurrection body. It was a permanent, not temporary arrangement. He also informed me that the expression had been at the heart of a heresy which had troubled the Church in previous times, proposing that Christ was only made man temporarily. Fortunately, I was in time to rewrite that line to 'dwells in humanity' before it was committed to tape.

Keeping the story central

I agree with Robert Webber when he writes, 'The content of Christian worship is Jesus Christ – his fulfilment of the Old Testament, his birth, life, death, resurrection, ascension and coming again.'[2] If we are not celebrating the 'Christ-event' at the heart of our worship, we are in serious danger of drifting in a sea of subjective experience.

The first song in the Bible celebrates an event in which a dramatic rescue took place, retelling the story of Israel's deliverance from Pharaoh at the Red Sea. This 'salvation story' is at the heart of Old Testament worship. But even that great deliverance was only a foreshadowing of a much greater salvation story, the coming of Jesus Christ who would lead his people from the slavery of sin and death to freedom, forgiveness and eternal life. Those who believe in him enter the story and become a part of it.

But how can we pack rich content into songs that are in a popular style? It has to be said that the rock-pop genre, into which category many worship choruses fit, is not always ideal for carrying extensive, deep, or content-rich lyrics. A good test of the balance of our worship content is whether it enables us to enjoy three dynamics, the presence of which, not coincidentally, are supremely evident in the celebration of the Lord's Supper:

(a) Re-enactment: we proclaim the historical event of Christ as revealed in the scriptures through the apostles and prophets.

(b) Realization: we participate now in Christ's death and resurrection by appropriating by faith the power and benefit of his finished work into our lives.

(c) Anticipation: we reach into the future in longing for the final fulfilment of God's plan to bring all things in heaven and earth under the headship of Christ, seizing hold by faith, hope and endurance to a kingdom in which death, sin and suffering will end, and Christ's eternal kingdom of justice and peace will reign for ever.

Qualities of good songs for congregational use

As I write, I bear in mind the limitations of songs for congregational use. Lyrics need to be characterized by:

(a) Accessibility: they are to be sung in public by a wide variety of people from an equally wide variety of cultural and educational backgrounds.

(b) Simplicity: they must rhyme and scan, and be capable of being understood in the time it takes to sing them.

(c) Theological integrity: they must not stray far from scripture and the imagery of devotion.

(d) Carrying conviction: they must be free from obscurities, doubts and ambiguities.

While I have a particular concern about content, I have to humbly recognize that much non-Western Christian music has long been characterized by simple music, driving beat, repetitive lyrics, light content and an emphasis on experience. This often expresses a vibrant committed faith. I have heard the opinion expressed that worship music should be judged not by the songs themselves but by the people who sing them. I tend to agree with the person who said that we must welcome any church music that helps produce disciples of Christ.

Worship music must be comprehensible to the culture in which it is formed and true to the unchanging gospel. It must be suitable for glorifying God, unifying believers and expressing doctrine. Melodies must be within a range suitable for male and female voices in unison. Intervals, syncopation and tempo must all be attainable by the average congregation.

The challenge and process of writing for worship

Once I have the first draft of a song, I regard it as an essential part of the songwriting process both to submit the song to trusted friends for critique and to test it on a group representative of those for whom it is intended. I will never forget presenting a song to one of our senior church leaders who, after a few valiant attempts at positive comment, posed the penetrating question: 'Can you think of an occasion when we would ever use this song, Graham?' Unfortunately I couldn't!

In the case of congregational praise and worship songs, I look for an opportunity to apply what I call the 'tonsil test' – to sing it in worship. Then we can ask questions. What happened when I taught it to the congregation? Did it 'work'? What vox-pop reaction did I get afterwards? Did it help people to give their worship? Did it teach truth? Did it only work well as a catchy melody, or as a performance? Was the lyric appreciated but the melody less so? It is important, of course, to judge it within the context in which it is intended to be used, for example a youth meeting, a family service, a Eucharist or an evangelistic gathering. If I feel it is necessary, which I frequently do, I then edit or rewrite the song. I have often drawn encouragement from the knowledge that Isaac Watts' hymn 'When I survey the wondrous cross' is a rewriting of an earlier text that was much inferior.

On a personal level, the future presents challenges which are not new, but which perhaps increase as one gets older. First, I recognize my need to be a worshipper, not a manufacturer of religious songs. To be a servant of God and of his people, I need to grow in a real and vital relationship with God the Father so that the creativity is an overflow of that relationship. I need to cultivate a sensitivity to the presence of God by living in such a way that I do not quench the Holy Spirit. I do not want to fall back onto natural gifting alone, but rather to grow in knowledge and understanding of the word of God, finding fresh insights that fuel the content and inspire the melodies.

Regarding technical challenges, as a non-technically trained musician it is very difficult for me to describe what they are – I just get stuck! To me it boils down to searching for what sounds 'right' or 'fresh', which are, of course, subjective terms. As a writer looking for melodies that are simple enough to be accessible to an average congregation, yet interesting, I find originality to be a particular challenge. I still remember playing the draft of a new song based on a psalm to some American publishers, who promptly fell about laughing. It transpired that I had innocently replicated the melody to an old American folk song to the words: 'The old grey mare, she ain't what she used to be, ain't what she used to be.'

Like every songwriter, I need to maintain musical creativity, to innovate, to break redundant musical habits and to find musical stimulation. In the midst of family, church and business responsibilities, I have to find time, freedom from distraction, fresh inspiration and renewed motivation. I also need to overcome the fear of failure, the intimidation of silence and the daunting challenge of a blank piece of paper! Recently, I realized that in my busyness I was losing the art of listening to music, and have begun to take steps to re-educate my ears. This can be used as excellent justification for purchasing a new hi-fi system!

My early songwriting was very spontaneous. It has since become a lot more conscious and deliberate. I can relate to the miner of gems who has, on average, to dig and process 25 tonnes of raw material in order to produce one carat of uncut and unpolished diamond. A preacher friend of mine commented that after decades of preaching and preparing sermons, and after teaching the same basic truths to several generations, what refreshes and motivates him is when fresh insights suddenly appear out of the discipline of study.

Hopes for the future

One of the contemporary factors which we should not undervalue as we look to the future is the freedom that we currently enjoy to innovate and experiment. The extent of this may be unprecedented in church history – certainly there has never been such opportunity to influence others, and be influenced by others, through the communications media that are available. I hope that music in the worship of the Church will be deeply rooted in the ancient truths of who God is and the revelation of the Father through Christ. I hope that it will flourish in the sunshine of God's manifest presence. We are the people of the presence, so we need music that is conceived in God's presence to equip the people to worship in God's presence.

I hope this worship will be the fruit of lives full of holiness and good works – lifestyles of worship, true worshippers. I hope it will be diverse in style, because it will take the whole Church in the whole world adequately to reflect the glory of Christ; and that the various cultural 'tribes' will unite as the true worshippers the Father is seeking, valuing one another's distinct contribution, yet not demanding that our styles and tastes should all be the same. I hope it will increase in excellence because of the 'alabaster jar' motive, in which we, like the woman whose worship Jesus accepted, give the best we have (Luke 7.36ff.).

I long for more songwriters of theological depth to emerge and give us a new wave of doctrinal hymns in contemporary styles, including music that expresses the greatness and majesty of God. We also need new scripture songs, songs that enable us to sing basic doctrinal truths, and songs based on biblical stories and characters. This would be a kind of Alpha Course in song! We need songs that propel the Church into mission and service; songs that prepare us for persecution, adversity and global uncertainty. I hope that neglected themes such as the Trinity, the priesthood of Christ, perseverance, heaven, hell, persecution, providence, work, suffering and lament will receive the attention they deserve.

In our public worship, I hope that we can find a greater balance between freedom and spontaneity on the one hand and order and structure on the other. I hope that, without losing their distinctives, different worship traditions will cross-pollinate and thereby strengthen each other.

I hope that more Christian composers will write and publish music of beauty and spiritual power, which overflows the walls of the Christian world and impacts the surrounding culture.

I hope that rather than despising, suspecting or fearing one another, different generations in the Church will value one another so much that ways will be found to worship together across divides of taste, style and culture, and that we will combine the best of the old and the best of the new.

Looking to the future, I believe there will be an increasing emphasis on extended gatherings for worship, and already many churches are engaged in twelve and twenty-four hour periods of unbroken worship and prayer. I anticipate that there will be centres where worship and prayer goes on day and night on a rota basis for periods of time, perhaps for years, perhaps until Christ returns. The main aim of this will be to go deeper into God's presence and to go deeper into worship, seeking to experience God's presence with an intensity that short meetings and busy lifestyles do not allow. Among many other things it will be a prophetic sign of the time when all of creation will be finally caught up in ceaseless worship, and where, from the rising of the sun to its setting, the world is once more totally given over to the worship of the creator (Psalm 113.3). A powerful stream of intercession will flow through these meetings, and prayer and worship will flow in and out of one another. Alongside this worship, there will be an increasing general emphasis on the presence of God, and a call to live constantly in his presence through the mundane things of life, and in the service of the poor.

I anticipate that the persecution of Christians will continue to increase as it did during the last century, and we will need songs which both prepare us for times of pressure and persecution and sustain us through them. I was very struck while reading a book on the underground church in China how many of their songs are about persecution and the cost of following Jesus, and celebrate the sufferings and martyrdom of the apostles of old.[3]

As natural disasters and man-made threats to the well-being of humanity continue, we need songs which express our trust in the sovereignty of God over creation and the affairs of the nations. Perhaps such songs will help to draw us away from the danger of becoming over-concerned with our individual spiritual well-being. I have long believed that the greatest stimulus to the worship life of the Church is mission and outreach. Worship flourishes in the context of church planting, community action, service of the poor, and prayer that reaches outwards to the needs of others. Worldwide prayer movements will continue to spawn songs born out of prayer, many of which songs will put prophetic prayers into the mouths and hearts of Christians.

Returning to Jesus' encounter with the Samaritan woman, her first act of true worship was to believe in Jesus. Her second was to spill out the news of the Messiah to her neighbours and friends, calling them to meet him for themselves.

John Piper began his book *Let the Nations Be Glad* with these words:

> Mission is not the ultimate goal of the church. Worship is. Missions exists because worship doesn't. Worship is ultimate, not missions, because God is ultimate, not man. When this age is over, and the countless millions of the redeemed fall on their faces before the throne of God, missions will be no more. It is a temporary necessity. But worship abides forever . . . But worship is also the fuel of missions. Passion for God in worship precedes the offer of God in preaching. You can't commend what you don't cherish. Missions begins and ends in worship.[4]

Never before has music had such a pervasive influence in the world as it does now. Millions turn to music for entertainment, relaxation, a sense of identity and belonging, and increasingly, spiritual enlightenment. Yet the world has heard very little music which is vibrant with truth, which is saturated with the power of the Holy Spirit, and which fulfils the purpose for which music was created: to glorify God and celebrate his greatest gift to humankind – Jesus Christ. It is time they did. Let's get to it!

8

The Lost Tradition of Lament

Introduction

On Wednesday 13 March 1996, at 9.30 in the morning, a
deranged gunman walked into a primary school in the cathedral town of Dunblane, Scotland, and opened fire on classes of
children in the school gymnasium, killing sixteen children
and one teacher. On Sunday 17 March 1996, throughout
Scotland, if not further afield, ministers and worship leaders of
all traditions were faced with a dilemma – how to reflect a
nation's anguish in liturgy and song.

Had the disaster happened at sea and involved fishermen,
the song immediately to hand would have been 'Eternal
Father, strong to save'. Had the disaster involved residents in
an old people's home, an appropriate hymn would surely
have been 'Abide with me'. Had it been a primarily rural constituency with the sons and daughters of the soil taken from
their habitat, metrical psalms and paraphrases would have
sprung to mind: 'The Lord's my Shepherd', or 'O God our
help in ages past', or 'I to the hills will lift mine eyes'.

But what do you sing when it is children? And what do you
sing when they are the innocent victims of cold-blooded
slaughter? And how do you represent the unspeakable
anguish in the hearts of their parents? And how do you reflect
the seeming impotence of religion to make sense of it all?

Three weeks after the killing of the children and their

teacher in Dunblane, I was at a clergy conference in Scotland
where, apropos the disaster, one minister from Aberdeen, a
devout and hospitable evangelical preacher stunned me with
the words: 'It was on that Sunday that I realized we had lost
the ability to lament.' It is odd that such a sentiment should
have been expressed in Scotland, for we have been and still are
a nation given to lament – the domination of Edinburgh by
Westminster; the perennial misfortunes of our football team
in the World Cup; the persistence of wet weather and midges
even into the third millennium. Scotland held on to metrical
psalmody, which Anglican England espoused for three hundred years after the Reformation but gradually displaced in
favour of chanted psalms in the mid-nineteenth century. And
within the metrical singing tradition – which was the sole and
mandatory tradition for most Protestants until the nineteenth
century – there were plentiful resources for lament. Scotland
also, unlike England, has had a greater reticence to be taken
over by the excesses of musical positivism in praise choruses
and charismatic songs. (Perhaps it is the weather!) Despite
this, the reality that faced this clergyman and many of his
counterparts was that there were no songs dealing with the
need to lament on that most horrible day.

The demise of the lament

I want to examine the reasons for this, and then to suggest
why the tradition of lament needs to be reinvigorated if not
redeemed.

Longevity

We live longer now that we used to. Or – to put it more
appropriately – people live longer nowadays than their fore-
bears did, given that we have all experienced two centuries
but few can claim three! A trip to any historic graveyard will

reveal that the average age of death for men and women today
is twenty years later than it was a century ago, and the graveyard inscriptions will also reveal that in rural as well as urban
Britain, child mortality soared in the nineteenth century. It
was partly to do with inadequate pre- and post-natal care; it
was partly to do with infestation and plagues – rickets, diph-
theria, smallpox; it was partly to do with malnutrition; it was
partly to do with the ravages of industrialization in terms of
unsanitary living and working conditions, child labour, etc; it
was also much to do with a political response of laissez-faire
regarding the lot of the urban poor.

But in such days the questions that did the rounds of every
street in which a child died were: 'Where is Arthur?' 'What
has happened to Thomasina?' 'What has happened to Mrs
Jackson's twins?' To that politically induced pastoral dilemma
answers, which children would understand, had to be given
regarding the afterlife. And so hymn writers and composers
laboured to produce words and music which would not so
much express anger and grief as look positively on the new
whereabouts of the deceased infants.

Songs arose, many of which have become almost icons of
private devotion, although they were originally intended for
use in times of grief:

If I come to Jesus, he will take my hand,
He will kindly lead me to a better land
There is a city bright
Closed are its gates to sin

Golden harps are sounding,
Angel voices ring

I'm a little pilgrim
And a stranger here

When he cometh, when he cometh
To take up his jewels

and even the revered:

Jesus loves me! He will stay
Close beside me all the way.
Then his little child will take
up to heaven for his dear sake.

Throughout the twentieth century not only did the rate of
child mortality decrease, but the increased longevity of adults
has meant that fewer people are 'taken' in their prime. More
and more of us live to an old age where the timeliness of death
– if it ever is timely – is more appropriate. There are – it may
be argued – fewer occasions that merit lamenting.

Shifting theological sands

I am aware that when I address the issue of theological shifts,
I am not so much getting into deep water as getting into a
variety of currents, different ones of which will resonate with
different people. Let me briefly identify three.

First, the notion of God as omnipotent, omniscient and
distant has been gradually displaced in favour of the God who
shares our lot, who is present within the community, who
forsakes untouchability. This is reflected in diverse phenom-
ena, such as the salutary theological reflections of Dietrich
Bonhoeffer who, during his incarceration, wrote of the God
who comes to us not as all-powerful, but 'when he is sore
bested'. In another sphere entirely, the documents of Vatican
II regarding the architecture of worship spaces, reorientated
the altar from standing over and apart from the congregation
to being the focus of attention and of Christ's presence in their
midst.

If God is distant, other-worldly and passive, there is a need
to try to move the heart of the Almighty by tears and impre-
cations. But if God is in our midst then our hymns which

reflect sorrow might even dare to be upbeat. Witness Brian Wren in his hymn 'Christ is alive':

> In every insult, rift or war
> Where colour, scorn or wealth divide,
> He suffers still, yet loves the more
> And lives though ever crucified.

Second, there is a slight awkwardness about heaven. Yuri Gagarin and all astronauts after him have not seen God above the clouds, a happy land with children walking hand in hand with Jesus, or legions of harp-strumming and nectar-quaffing saints. Indeed we so positively determined the topography and location of heaven in previous centuries, and we so over-populated it with children, that it has become a bit of an embarrassment. So, from C. H. Dodd on, we have gone for 'realized eschatology' – a sense of the presentness of heaven on earth, at the expense of detracting attention from whether there is or might be some sphere of divine association or inner presence which subsumes those who die in faith. It is very rare in post-war hymn texts to have a focus on the afterlife.

The third theological shift is a move from the metanarrative to the soundbite; from a declaration of the overarching purposes of God to a need to deal succinctly with the problem to hand but never put it in a larger context. This, the politically correct may take to be an effect of postmodernism.

One of my favourite passages of scripture is Job 38. It comes at the end of a long sequence of moral and theological investigations into the lot of Job who has been dealt raw deal after raw deal, and who does not understand why this has happened. After Job has complained and his friends have tried to justify his suffering and the ways of God, it is time for God to speak personally.

> Who is this who darkens counsel
> with words devoid of knowledge?

Brace yourself and stand up like a man;
I shall put questions to you and you must answer.

Where were you when I laid the earth's foundations?
Tell me, if you know and understand . . .
On what do its supporting pillars rest?
Who set its corner stone in place? . . .

Who supported the sea at its birth? . . .
Which is the way to the home of light? (Job 38.1-19 REB)

And so on, until Job is pummelled into silence.

What is happening is that God is putting the mystery of Job's personal suffering in the context of the metanarrative of the mysteries of providence and grace. Job is challenged to see the unfathomable nature of what has happened to him in the context of the unfathomable nature of all creation.

But in a world which has been weaned away from the big picture into snap-shots, instant answers are wanted, not long-term perspectives.

A loss of liturgical integrity

The hymnodic equivalent of this is a move away from texts that articulate the complexities of human life and God's engagement in it to choruses. But few choruses were made for singing at funerals, coming as they often do from a success theology background where everything good happens to the elect of God and if anything bad happens, it is a sign of apostasy.

If some one asks me what I think of choruses and praise-songs, I normally say that I don't mind them as long as they are true to biblical faith, applicable for corporate use and not produced primarily for commercial gain. In another context I would gladly elaborate on these criteria. Here I deal with them briefly.

Biblical verifiability

Any song that is proposed for use by God's people should be true to biblical faith. This does not mean that it directly quotes from scripture, but that it reflects the panoply of divine initiative and human response that we find in the scriptures. I do not find this in most chorus books, which concentrate attention on the majesty of God and the exaltation of Jesus at the expense of dealing with Christ's humanity, the expression of anger, doubt, bewilderment and sorrow, which inhabits a third of the Psalms, and the prophetic injunctions on matters of social justice.

Corporate provenance

While faith in God is a matter of personal commitment, it is also a corporate reality. We are not joined to our Maker by private cellular phone links; we are incorporated into the body of Christ the efficacy of which is known when members rejoice or lament in empathy with others. It strikes me that an unhealthy proportion of praise songs and choruses use the first person singular and witness to a highly subjective relationship with God which has no room for shared faith or mutual accountability.

It is also notable that some of those who, in a previous era, were keen to dispense with the tyranny of the organist and choir because they did not let the people sing, are now fulfilling the arrogant and elitist roles they previously denounced, as the worship of God's people becomes dominated by amplification which highlights the performer's skill, and overhead projectors which forbid any deep engagement with the text being sung.

Not primarily for commercial advantage

It is right and proper that people who expend their talents for the benefit of the Church should be remunerated as writers or composers. But the prior question is whether work is written for mass circulation and commercial gain, or whether it is written for these people in this place, out of this particular experience irrespective of whether or not it be sung again. It is disquieting to teach occasionally at summer schools for hymn writers, which I do in the USA, and find that the recurrent question is 'How can I get published?' There is already a popular music industry dedicated to producing musical monosodium glutamate, which leaves the listeners wanting more of the same, without Christian musicians emulating that kind of pap.

The need for lament

So much for some of the causes of a decline in the singing of songs of lament. Now, more positively, I would like to suggest some reasons for its revival . . . and do so in parallel with the categories I alluded to above – pastoral, theological and musical.

Pastoral considerations

Hymnody and church music, as much as their chief end is to glorify God, also have a profound pastoral significance – the fulfilment of which is undoubtedly one of the unique ways in which they glorify God. For it is within the purposes of hymnody and church music to speak for God to the people, and for the people to God; to make with integrity the connection between the human and the divine which prose and direct speech cannot always manage. That is why an anthem such as Weelkes' *When David Heard that Absalom was Slain* or John Tavener's *Song for Athene* sung at the funeral of the Princess of Wales have the capability of moving people beyond the realms of sentimentality into a holistic expression of grief.

Five years ago, I met in Grand Rapids, Michigan, a woman who had grown up in a Roman Catholic family in central Scotland and left home in the 1960s to travel in the Far East. She eventually became the partner of a young American man who took her back to his home town. Not long after arriving in Grand Rapids, she – Shona – went along to a Protestant charismatic church where she was converted. All were thrilled for her. Soon after, she brought her partner and he was converted. Everyone praised the Lord. Six months later they decided to get married in church and the congregation were head over heels in Hallelujahs. A year after their marriage she gave birth to their first child, and the church could not contain its joy at how God had blessed this favoured and chosen couple.

A year later she had a miscarriage, and the following year she had a stillborn baby. And the church kept back, and some began to conjecture whether this might not be God's way of recompensing them for their earlier years living together out of wedlock. At that time she could not go near her church. She could not participate in an orgy of charismatic fervour when her heart and soul were laid low.

I asked her what had kept her in faith – for she was clearly a woman of faith. And she spoke of how one day in her darkest despair, she remembered words she had learned in Latin as a child growing up in the pre-Vatican II Roman Catholic Church: *De profundis clamavi*. And remembering it was a psalm, she turned to the Psalter and found at number 130:

Out of the depths I call to you, O Lord.
Lord hear my prayer, and let your ear be
attentive to the voice of my pleading.

And she discovered other psalms which spoke of where she was in language which she might not have dared to offer to God on her own behalf. For her the truth became real that sometimes we will never be able to sing Hallelujah unless we have cried out

'How long?'
and 'How long?'
and 'Why have you turned your back on me, O Lord?'

It is not so much that the articulation of this sense of despair and abandonment will bring an automatic answer. The assurance comes much more in knowing that such things can be said by us and are heard by God.

I could give innumerable examples of people for whom growth of faith has been dependent on the articulation of reality, and who have known moments when the hymnody and music of the Church simply failed them.

Let me speak of one – a young man in Glasgow who told me his story a while after the pain had begun to abate.

He and his wife were looking forward to the birth of their first child, when in the third month of pregnancy, after a scan they were told that the child was deformed and were given the option of a termination. They declined and decided to have the baby. After eight months and other scans, they were told – in genuine kindness – that the baby was so severely deformed that the trauma of birth would probably cause it to die . . . and they had to be prepared for that. So they decided to have the birth by Caesarean section. Thus the baby was born, and named Jennifer, and held in her parents' arms until she died an hour after birth.

Stunned and grieved and angered by all this, as the couple were, what compounded their sorrow was not having anything to sing at the child's funeral that represented where they were before God. And, because this experience of losing a child by miscarriage or perinatal death affects almost one in five sets of parents, their sense of abandonment by the liturgy of the Church is not isolated.

A while after meeting the bereft father, I wrote a text based on what I remembered from our conversation:

> We cannot care for you the way we wanted,
> Or cradle you or listen to your cry;
> But, separated as we are by silence,
> Love will not die.
>
> We cannot watch you growing into childhood
> And find a new uniqueness every day;
> But for special as you would have been among us,
> You still will stay.
>
> We cannot know the pain or the potential
> Which passing years would summon or reveal;
> But for that true fulfilment Jesus promised
> We hope and feel.
>
> So through the mess of anger, grief and tiredness,
> Through tensions which are not yet reconciled,
> We give to God the worship of our sorrow
> And our dear child.
>
> Lord, in your arms which cradle all creation
> We rest and place our baby beyond death,
> Believing that she now, alive in heaven,
> Breathes with your breath.[1]

Theological honesty

It is simply demeaning to God and dishonest to the people of God to portray the Maker and Saviour of the world solely in terms of distant transcendence as suggested by Renaissance and Baroque anthems, or in terms of ephemeral jollity as implied by some contemporary praise choruses. We can either have all of God or none of God. God is not interested in offering only the preferred side of the divine reality to worshippers. That is a biblical fact to which the Old Testament gives eloquent witness. Time after time, the people of God imagine that they have their picture of their Maker right, and then God changes the picture. Time after time they produce what is considered to be appropriate liturgy, and then God tells them that it is a sham. There is always more to God than we can imagine, and not every glimpse of our Maker, not every word of our Saviour will be to our best liking. Indeed, when did God ever say that the Church should be a pleasure zone or discipleship a bed of roses, or worship a happy hour imbibing cheaply of the Spirit?

Church music is invariably a matter of subjective choice – what is possible in this building with these people and this choir? But given that, it always must attempt to represent to the people a God who will not be constrained by our limitations or predilections. That, to some extent, is the beauty of the Anglican daily offices which require, come hail or shine, that all the psalms will be sung or said in rotation and that even the awkward and embarrassing lines of scripture will be given an airing – even if no one is there to hear. But in the absence of a cathedral tradition with sung offices – which is the reality for most worshippers though it is still regarded in places as the litmus test which the majority can never pass – the hymnody of the Church has to ensure that there is a balanced diet not just of humanity's yearning and praise for God, but of God's injunctions and yearning for humanity.

And in the midst of all this, there will be moments when hymnody has to express God's sorrow . . . for God sometimes has tears on his cheek; and there will be moments when sometimes hymnody will express God's bewilderment – for God sometimes is at odds as to what to do with the people;

and there will be moments when sometimes hymnody expresses God's anger. The text of the Orthodox Trisagion does this very well.

Liturgical integrity

Good music is a deep thing. Like good poetry, it can be explored time and time again and delivers something of freshness with each performance, and accrues all the while layers of association and fondness. That is as applicable to melodies as it is to symphonies. If one considers what Vaughan Williams did in his 'Dives and Lazarus' variations, with the tune 'Kingsfold' which is beloved of Guinness-drinkers in County Down, you can feel for the magnificence of that gentle folk tune. More contemporarily, James MacMillan's percussion concerto *Veni, Veni, Immanuel* – now reckoned to be one of the most frequently played post-war concertos which received its 200th performance in Newcastle recently – is an example of how that magnificent melody associated with the Advent antiphons is marvellously rich and exploitable.

This quality in good music of being deep is, I would venture, applicable across musical thresholds. It is a truth known in the writing of Lennon and McCartney as in the African-American canon of spirituals as in the symphonic writing of Brahms or Bruckner. That range of layered depth is what allows music modestly to claim that it is both a metaphor for and communicator of divine grace.

But music only achieves that quality when it is either honed in the fires of communal use – as is the case with folk tune, or when it is the product of a mind which forsakes not simplicity but shallowness, and is open to the heights and depths of intellectual insight and emotional experience. Not to deal with the depths of life in the writing of music is to court shallowness in the composer and to disenfranchise the congregation or listeners from that which makes life rich and real.

9

The Future of the Hymn

JANET WOOTTON

Introduction

'The future of the hymn' – that might be considered to be a
rather optimistic title! For a large number of church-going
Christians, hymns are boring and old-fashioned, while the
vast majority of the population never have the opportunities
to sing and become familiar with hymns which existed in
former years. We are into the third generation of people
who have had no contact with Christian worship, beyond
christenings, weddings and funerals. During twenty years of
Christian ministry, I have seen a generation that had to ask
granny for the choice of hymns for the wedding service
replaced by a generation that doesn't understand what the
word 'hymn' means.

My own gloomy premonition is confirmed by two writers
on the subject of hymnody, who, like me, clearly have a great
affection for the form, but can see the hymn culture disappearing. Donald Webster, in a lecture given to the Church Music
Society, warns, 'Sadly there isn't much time left. As congregations decline numerically, and a generation that has been given
the opportunity to love its hymnody passes, those who are left
will be unable to carry the torch, because they have been given
no opportunity to experience this heritage for themselves'.[1]

Richard Watson, Professor of English at Durham, has written the classic text on the English hymn, but ends with a

section containing this sentence: 'I have written this book in the hope of earning some respect for the hymn while it is still a part of a popular culture, before it becomes a subject of study for Church historians and antiquarians.'[2] I worked with Richard Watson on the committee that compiled the Methodist and ecumenical hymn book, *Hymns and Psalms* (1983), and have shared a platform with him since then. In all his writing and speaking, his deep love of hymns shines out. If someone as affectionately knowledgeable about hymns as he can write of their imminent demise as a popular form, the picture is gloomy indeed.

Modern church music is perceived as being choruses or charismatic songs, led sometimes by small music groups, sometimes by highly professional groups or bands. For many, the organist and congregation, or even the piano and congregation, joined together in song is a thing of the past.

On the other hand, the exponents of the hymn regard modern Christian music as unremittingly facile and completely without content. 'Old' is hymns and 'new' is choruses. Between the two there exists an extreme hostility. Organists walk out; certain sections of the congregation stand grim and tight-lipped if the new books are in use; others plod resignedly through well-known and well-loved hymns, despising them precisely because they are well-known and loved by the 'traditionalists'.

In the middle – rather uncomfortably in the middle – of all this, there exists a small band of modern hymn writers, writing good new texts and tunes in the tradition of the hymn, not the song, chorus or chant, but writing in the modern idiom. Unless they are cruelly mistaken, the hymn has a future and it is, at least partly, in their hands.

In this paper, the word 'hymn' means words with music for congregational singing in worship, generally addressed to God and expressing the experience of the singers. It is pretty well impossible to draw a firm line between hymns and songs, though hymns differ from choruses in generally having a series of verses over which the theological sense of the hymn develops.

How did hymns arise and what job did they do?

Controversy and outright hostility is not foreign to the field of hymnody. In fact, the English hymn was forged in the raging fires of the Reformation. Far from simply spotting a need and filling it, Isaac Watts, known as the 'father' of English hymnody, knowingly entered a battlefield fraught with danger.

At the time of the Reformation in England, the singing of hymns was regarded as heretical or dangerous on several fronts. For one thing, while Luther recommended and even wrote hymns for use in worship – the poet Heine called 'Ein feste Burg' the 'Marseillaise Hymn of the Reformation'[3] – Calvin regarded singing in worship as part of the splendour and ritual of Rome, to be stripped away from true and spiritual worship. The English Reformation largely adopted a Calvinistic approach.

Specific to England was the battle over uniformity. While the singing of Psalms could be regulated, so that every parish used the same material on the same days, hymn texts were ungovernable and invited diversity or even dissent. In 1559, the new Act of Uniformity was augmented by a set of royal injunctions, which included the allowance:

> that there be a modest distinct song, so used in all parts of the common prayers in the church, that the same may be understood, as if it were read without singing, and yet, nevertheless, for the comforting of such that delight in Music, it may be permitted that in the beginning, or in the end of common prayers, either at morning or evening, there may be sung an hymn, or such like song, to the praise of Almighty God, in the best sort of melody and

music that may be conveniently devised, having respect that the sentence of the hymn may be understood and perceived.[4]

There was much argument about the meaning of the injunction and what, precisely, it permitted. Generally, the singing of hymns other than metrical psalms was discouraged in conforming churches.

Among nonconformist dissenters, that is the outlawed groups that developed into Congregationalists, Presbyterians and Baptists, among others, the argument was about the propriety of singing words written by humans, rather than the word of God. Psalms could be versified, though even this was suspect, but no human poetry could add to or improve on what God's Spirit had ordained.

These were not academic or esoteric debates. They raged through the pages of pamphlets and books, divided congregations and families, and provided a focus for the religious and civil struggles of the time. And, in a far more dangerous era, hymn writers were again right in the middle of the battle.

Isaac Watts, the son of a Dissenter who had been imprisoned for his beliefs, not only published settings of the Psalms, but also set his hand to a wider range of compositions. It is worth looking closely at the ways in which this powerful writer interpreted scripture through hymns.

The first text, 'High in the heavens, eternal God', is a setting of Psalm 36.5–9, and is taken from his book *The Psalms of David* published in 1719. His poetic setting shows his own wide knowledge of scripture. For example, the Psalm likens God's righteousness to the mountains and his justice to the deep – righteousness and justice are frequently paired in the Hebrew scriptures – but Watts picks up the description of the mountains in Wisdom literature, with their roots and foundations, and brings Wisdom writing's fascination with the wonders of creation into the imagery of the Psalm.[5]

The last verse of the hymn draws on the lovely imagery of the Psalm almost word for word, and yet fills out the imagery with a sure poetic touch. 'Rich and free' is not simply a line filler, but describes the fountain of life which comes from God, and the last line interprets the light in terms of the promise of God, fulfilled, so the singer understands, in the experience of salvation through Jesus Christ.

A second hymn, 'God is a name my soul adores', from *Horae Lyricae* (1706), demonstrates a move away from the single scripture passage towards a general theological or doctrinal text, drawing on a wide range of scripture. These are tremendous, powerful words, describing the very nature of God – the great original, the one who created all things by his word. The line, 'bade the waves roar, the planets shine' is lovely to sing, with its slight inversion of metre. Nothing like God appears through all his 'spacious' works.

The hymn is uncompromising. 'None but thy word can speak thy name.' This final line is no happy ending – this is about God, not about the worshipper, who is left in awestruck silence at the end. Humanity is purely submissive, even the thrones and dominions. Our world is described in words we no longer – though we might like to – sing: 'This little dwelling place of worms.'

By the way, apart from the omission of that, and other verses, recent compilers have made a tiny, but significant alteration. In the first verse, God is the infinite (lower case) Unknown (upper case) – Unknown is the noun, and infinite the adjective. It is now more normally printed, 'the Infinite (upper case) unknown (lower case). Rather than the Unknown, God is now the Infinite, which is not the tenor of the rest of the hymn.

Watts intended his hymns to be generally useful. He claimed that they were in no way sectarian, and gave permission to congregations, if they found any word to be doctrinally offensive, to alter it at will. However, there is, in his use of the word 'saints', an often deliberate exposition of the New Testament meaning of the word, that is, the whole people of God, the redeemed, rather than individuals whose lives and works are recognized as an example to others.

This can be seen from the first of Watts' two hymns that I have cited. While the Psalm simply celebrates God's general bounty to living things, Watts adds God's special, 'peculiar' care for 'saints'. Watts' doctrine of sainthood arises from time to time in his writing. One of his communion hymns begins with the words, 'Jesus invites his saints/ To sit around his board', and completes the first verse with a description of the saints, 'Here pardon'd rebels (we now sing, 'sinners') sit and hold/ Communion with their Lord'. The saints are those who are singing the hymn – the gathered congregation – there only by God's pardon for their rebellion.

Watts' *Hymns and Spiritual Songs* (1707), a title which, set against the controversy of the time, deliberately omits 'Psalms' from the much disputed text from Colossians 3.16, went through a huge number of editions, and became a standard collection of hymns for use in churches. Much later, other writers tentatively followed. The Baptist Anne Steele's hymns, now no longer sung, were very popular in the late eighteenth century. Philip Doddridge, a congregational minister, gave us 'Hark the glad sound, the Saviour comes', and 'O happy day that fixed my choice on thee my saviour and my God', a hymn which has been theologically and poetically ruined by the addition of a nineteenth-century chorus. William Cowper and John Newton wrote a collection called *The Olney Hymns* (1779), many of which are still sung.

Then came the Methodist revival, and the nature and purpose of hymn writing changed radically. John and Charles Wesley drew inspiration from hearing the fervent songs of a group of Moravian Brethren, whose hymnic tradition drew from the Lutheran Reformation and had no hint of Calvinistic hesitation about the place of music in Christian worship. Rather, they used hymns both to inspire and to teach. The texts carry strong doctrinal, even sometimes polemic messages, and are filled with a rich sense of spiritual fervour.

John Wesley made several translations of Moravian texts, one of which is the well-known 'Jesus, thy blood and right-eousness'. Wesley translated only 24 of Zinzendorf's 33 stanzas, and various selections have been made from them for different hymn books. The dramatic text carries an uncom-promising theology of salvation by grace – the precious blood of Jesus, whose life and death are the only plea in the face of judgment – through faith – all the singer does is to affirm, 'Lord, I believe'.

But John and Charles Wesley espoused a rather different theology. Certainly salvation by grace through faith rings out loud and clear in many of their texts, for example, the excit-ing and profound, 'And can it be that I should gain an interest in the Saviour's blood'. But Methodism believed that the Christian could achieve and grow in perfection in this life, the doctrine of Arminianism. Charles Wesley, in particular, intended his hymns to teach and persuade of this doctrine. It comes out in a fervent desire not only to lay claim on Jesus' righteousness, but to be filled with righteousness and holiness.

The hymn, 'Love divine, all loves excelling' ends with a yearning for perfection which links this world with the world to come: 'Finish then thy new creation, pure and spotless (originally 'sinless') let us be', and a now usually omitted verse makes the point quite plainly with its powerful line, 'Take away the power of sinning'. Amen!

Charles Wesley quite deliberately used his hymn texts to carry his theology, and, unlike Watts, forbade the alteration of his texts in any way. He also produced a hymn book, *A Collection of Hymns for the Use of the People Called Methodists* (1780), which set out to be the standard book in use. It was intended to be within the financial reach of every member of a congregation, and to replace the bewildering variety of hymn collections around at the time. The preface made two bold claims, to contain 'a proper collection of hymns for general use, carefully made out of all these books', and to encompass 'all the important truths of our most holy religion, whether speculative or practical'. For the first time, the hymns are ordered thematically for practical use. In other words, this is the first hymn book in the modern sense of the word.

While Wesley's Arminian doctrine was propounded in his hymns, Augustus Toplady, among others, took up the opposing cause, writing hymns which push the pure Calvinist position: 'Rock of Ages cleft for me' first appeared as a quatrain, in an article entitled 'Life, a journey' in the *Gospel Magazine* of October 1775, edited at the time by Toplady.

> Rock of Ages cleft for me,
> Let me hide myself in thee;
> Foul I to the fountain fly,
> Wash me, Saviour, or I die.

There followed two articles of biting satire directed mainly at John Wesley. The hymn, with its 'Could my zeal no respite know' in the second verse and 'Nothing in my hand I bring' in the third, echoes Luther's 'Out of the depths I cry to thee' and serves to emphasize the theology of salvation only by God's grace. Theological controversy was still finding a home in hymnody.

Wesley's preaching and his hymns had an enormous effect. In fact, during the eighteenth and nineteenth centuries, hymns as a liturgical form had an effect far beyond anything we can understand today. Richard Arnold writes, 'Unlike today, in the eighteenth century the hymn was probably the most widely read and memorized literary/verbal structure of all; in its almost incredible popularity it would have become part of the consciousness and the daily and weekly lives of more people in England than any other genre.'[6] The power of hymnody is largely unrecognized, and the hymn texts being sung by congregations and in schools, and learnt by children and adults both through usage and in classes, have a potential to describe the thinking of ordinary people which has been largely unrealized.

Susan S. Tamke makes the same point about the nineteenth century:

> It seems indisputable that quantitatively the effect of hymns on the Victorian public was more profound than the literary works which traditionally have been mined so assiduously by cultural historians. In sheer volume, the writing of hymns far outweighed the writing of poetry in the nineteenth century. More important, the people whose lives were affected by hymns far outnumber those who were affected by poetry . . . hymns were sung everywhere – on street corners, at secular meetings, in the nursery, as well as in churches and chapels.[7]

At the end of the eighteenth century, hymn writing was poised to take off. Throughout the nineteenth century, the plethora of religious movements in Britain and America each gave rise to a distinctive stream of hymn writing.

The Salvation Army along with Sankey and Moody produced earnest hymns calling on the singer to come to Jesus, to accept a total change of life and, once there, to count their blessings and rest in the blessed assurance which watched and looked from above.

The two hymns cited in that paragraph are famous. 'Count your blessings' is still loved and sung in some settings. It counsels acceptance of the singer's present lot, not to hanker after lands and gold, not to be disheartened, but to do two things: to count the present blessings, which will be found to outnumber any disadvantages there may be; and to look forward to 'your reward in heaven and your home on high'. While this hymn was, and still is, a great comfort to many, its emphasis on acceptance and a classic 'pie in the sky when you die' sentiment is exactly the kind of language that gave rise to Marx's view of religion as the opiate of the people.

Frances van Alstyne's 'Blessed Assurance' is theologically more solid, and describes the blessed state of assurance of salvation. The hymn has an almost mystical quality, leading the singer further into the state of submission and rest with each verse. Van Alstyne, also known under her maiden name as Fanny Crosby, was an enormously prolific writer, accredited with some 8,000 texts under a variety of pseudonyms. She, and other writers of the nineteenth-century evangelical revival, provided for a hunger for new worship material – and in this context this means hymns – to convert and confirm the thousands who were coming to Christ in the English-speaking world.

In opposition to this enthusiastic singing, many in England were trying to raise the standard of church music and hymnody. The minister of my own church, Union Chapel, Islington, Henry Allon, used to run psalmody classes for the whole congregation of a thousand and more during the week, and expected a wide range of high quality music from the congregation on a Sunday.

In the Church of England, the Oxford Movement argued that the Thirty-Nine Articles of faith were not incompatible with Roman Catholicism. John Henry Newman, perhaps the most prolific writer in this tradition, like many others, eventually converted to Rome.

Another high churchman, John Mason Neale, led the rediscovery of Latin and Greek texts, making translations for congregational use. He gave us 'O come, O come Immanuel', from an eighteenth-century Latin text, 'Blessed City, heavenly Salem', originating in the sixth or seventh century and, 'The day of resurrection' from the Greek liturgy in the Pentecostarion.

Neale's translation of *Urbs Beata*, 'Blessed City', is typically strong. Again, the text and translation have gone through a number of versions, and this is a compilation of verses. The English words are dense and intellectually satisfying. The text draws on a picture of worship on earth as a reflection of the worship of heaven, and makes use of a number of scripture passages. 'Consubstantial, co-eternal' is not in the Latin text, but it is great fun to sing!

In the mean time, Catherine Winkworth was discovering the richness and evangelical fervour of German hymns. Another prolific translator, she sought to bring both the wealth and the inspiration of the hymns to English-speaking congregations. In the preface to *Lyra Germanica*, she wrote, 'the singing of hymns forms a much larger and more important part of public worship in the German Reformed Churches than in our own services. It is the mode by which the whole congregation is enabled to bear its part in the worship of God, answering in this respect to the chanting of our own Liturgy'.[8] She might have looked to the nonconformist and free churches of her own time to discover that that was exactly the function of hymns in their worship. Without Catherine Winkworth, we would not have 'Praise to the Lord, the Almighty, the King of Creation', or 'Now thank we all our God', among others.

There are many, many other writers of the nineteenth century. A little-known battle of the hymn books was going on in Unitarianism in England and America. In America, the Quaker John Greenleaf Whittier wrote some of our most loved hymns, including 'Dear Lord and Father of mankind'.

And there was a great upsurge in writing for children. The psychology of this writing, and the picture it gives of a Victorian childhood, is a study in itself. Richard Watson speaks of 'Katherine Hankey's regressive and infantile posturing' in 'Tell me the old, old story', and of the 'Threatening, sadistic, bullying, regressive, self-centred' tone of some others![9]

But one writer, an Irish Anglican vicar's wife, wrote a series of hymns for children which are loved – and hated – to this day. Cecil Frances Alexander was determined to set out the main tenets of Christian doctrine in a form that children could understand. So the incarnation is set forth in 'Once in royal David's city' with its injunction upon children to be 'mild, obedient, good as he'. The cross finds expression in 'There is a green hill far away'.

When it came to the wonders and orderliness of creation, Alexander wrote, 'All things bright and beautiful'. Two verses are now generally omitted. Verse six, which includes 'The rushes by the water/ We gather every day' recalls a childhood known by very few, if any, children today, though I can myself remember gathering rushes by the water. But verse three is a different matter altogether. Like 'Count your blessings' which counsels acquiescence in the face of poverty, 'All things bright and beautiful' accepts the order of wealth and poverty ('The rich man in his castle,/ and the poor man at his gate') as part of God's created order, which God gave us eyes to see, and lips to praise him for.

This theology was by no means universally accepted, though it was largely the theology which was sung in churches. Susan Tamke notes a reaction to the theology of acquiescence in writing about social justice:

> By the third and fourth decades of the (nineteenth) century, however, paralleling the growth of social and industrial unrest in England, hymns began to appear in newspapers and privately published hymnbooks vigorously demanding social justice. . . By following these changes in popularly published hymns, we can identify the extent to which England's transformed economic and social conditions were appreciated and assimilated by society in general. By tracing these changes in the denominational hymnals, we can identify the shift in social thinking in one of society's most conservative institutions, the church.[10]

By the beginning of the twentieth century, hymns on social themes were beginning to be accepted. G. K. Chesterton published 'O God of earth and altar' in *The Commonwealth*, a monthly periodical of the Christian Social Union, in 1915. Henry Scott Holland's 'Judge eternal throned in splendour' had appeared in the same periodical in 1904.

'O God of earth and altar' is interesting, since it uses deliberately archaizing language ('The walls of gold entomb us,/ The swords of scorn divide') to speak of issues that are current even today, and were even truer of the beginning of the last century. Verse two refers to political corruption, misuse and sale of arms, and the vast indifference of most people. 'The prince and priest and thrall' is a reference to the medieval classes of society, yet the words have the power to move.

Rudyard Kipling also wrote hymns of social justice, and even of warning, though we no longer sing them. He writes with what Richard Watson calls, 'the vatic power to assume the role that is granted to very few, that of the Old Testament prophet'.[11] The hymn, 'God of our fathers' is far more specific to its own time, but sounds a timely warning to the arrogance of the British empire at the beginning of its decline. The ringing, 'Lest we forget – lest we forget' recalls secular authorities and powers to the authority and power of God.

Issues facing hymn writers

I have lived through what has felt like a most exciting and creative period in hymn writing. By the beginning of the second half of the twentieth century, the world was changing. Two world wars, the horrors of Auschwitz and Hiroshima were known to a horrified human race, and complacency, though an ideal of the 1950s, was not really an option.

The 1960s and 1970s saw a new kind of writing in the folk revival. I can remember discovering and singing these with terrific seriousness. Here were hymns, or at least songs, which addressed the issues I was facing, or liked to think I was facing. Sydney Carter wrote with a light touch, but theological depth, not only 'Lord of the dance' but 'Friday morning' and 'The vicar is a beatnik'!

'Friday morning' is shattering to sing. It is put into the mouth of the thief who was crucified with Jesus, and spoke up for him to the other thief, and is as vigorous a challenge to theodicy as you might hope to meet. The songs published by Galliard, a forward-looking and daring publishing enterprise of Bernard Braley, one of the directors of Stainer & Bell, dealt with issues such as drug abuse, homelessness, racism (this was the period of post-war immigration from the West Indies), war and peace, and so on. *Faith Folk & Clarity*[12] is organized with half the songs on traditional Christian themes, and half on themes of Freedom and Prejudice, Peace and War, World Need and Social Concerns.

In the Roman Catholic Church, the Second Vatican Council of the 1970s brought about a revolution in worship styles – though many would say not enough of a revolution. In particular, having no great corpus of traditional English hymns, nor a three-hundred-year-old tradition of English liturgical language, the Roman Catholic Church was able to embrace a new hymnody. Estelle White might well be thought to have single-handedly provided the new hymns.

I had the privilege to interview Estelle recently. Of her writing, she said, 'Poetry writing is very different from hymn writing. Hymns have to be technically very precise. You can spread yourself as a poet. But the poetic and musical range in hymns has to be accessible. The congregation have to be able to sing it, and not have to ask "What do they mean?" all the time.'

One of the great issues confronting hymn writers in every age is how to write for this very particular and specific use. Hymns have to be accessible to a congregation at a first singing, without losing integrity or poetic quality. As great a name as Tennyson wrote, 'A good hymn is the most difficult thing in the world to write. In a good hymn you have to be commonplace and poetical. The moment you cease to be commonplace and put in any expression at all out of the common, it ceases to be a hymn.'[13]

This is a most difficult balance to strike. The best hymns are not only accessible, but give more each time of singing. My own experience of growing up with hymns is that I learnt the way along my own Christian journey as hymn words became true. As a child, I loved, 'O for a closer walk with God' for the verse, 'The dearest idol I have known, whate'er that idol be, help me to tear it from thy throne and worship only thee.' I was so young that I had to ask what an idol was! Later, I learnt to persevere from 'Father hear the prayer we offer, not for ease that prayer shall be, but for strength'. The great hymns increase in meaning as they go.

The marvellous thing about the last few decades is that great hymns are still being written. The greatest have the integrity and strength of the hymn tradition with the intellectual honesty and radical edge of the folk revival.

Among these are new settings of the Magnificat. The first is Fred Kaan's folk setting ('Sing we the song of high revolt'), to the tune of 'The Red Flag', published in 1968. This caused a bit of an outcry, because it called people to revolt and fight. The text drew uncompromisingly on the radical message of the Magnificat, and linked it to people's ordinary lives – 'crowded street and council flat' was a line much derided in its time.

Opposite this is Fred Kaan's much later 'Come! Sing and live a world Magnificat', written for the new millennium. Now the radical message is not so closely linked with the words of the Magnificat, but makes reference to different sections of scripture and even to other hymns (Lest we forget!). The language is far more sophisticated and the social message more informed.

Timothy Dudley Smith comes from a different tradition,

and his Magnificat ('Tell out, my soul, the greatness of the Lord!'), widely known and sung, focuses on Mary's praise of God. The hungry and the poor appear in only one line, and the language has a far more traditional feel to it.

The last is my own 'Moratorium on Magnificat', written after attending the service in Westminster Abbey for the 50th anniversary of Christian Aid. Michael Taylor, the then director of Christian Aid, gave the sermon. He spoke powerfully about the poor of the world, in contrast with the rich and powerful, personified in the Queen, Queen Elizabeth, who was there at the service. He looked straight at her, and said, 'There are some rich people in this church, some very rich people', and he said that we ought to declare a moratorium on singing the Magnificat until some of its radical message begins to be fulfilled.

Fred Kaan's early text is typical in a sense of the songs of the 1960s. It was printed in one of the short collections that were around at the time: *New Life*, published by Galliard in 1971. During the 1960s and 1970s, several short collections of experimental songs were published. As well as Galliard, Kevin Mayhew and Jubilate were publishing new writers. Denominational publishers also began to compile 'supplements' to hymn books, the most adventurous of which was the United Reformed Church's *New Church Praise* (1975).

The stage was set for two new kinds of development. First, a series of new denominational hymn books was brought out, beginning with the Methodist and (over-optimistically) ecumenical *Hymns and Psalms* of 1983. The question began to be asked, which of the new songs were of lasting value, enough to be included in a large, official collection of hymns. Interestingly, in *Hymns and Psalms*, 'Make me a channel of your peace', and some others from the charismatic revival, were included, but Sydney Carter's 'Lord of the dance' was thought to be ephemeral.

As hymn books began to be compiled, the issue of altering

texts arose. Some compilations changed the 'thee' form of address to 'you' throughout, and altered some other archaic language. The other reason for alteration was where language was non-inclusive, changing 'men' and 'man' wherever possible. This is a very difficult area. The suggestion is that hymns written in old-fashioned or exclusive language will not communicate, or will communicate the wrong things, in today's congregations. For my part, I will happily alter exclusive language, where this is possible with poetic integrity, since this is to right a wrong, as I will argue later. On the other hand, I would leave the 'thees' and 'thous' as examples of writing of their time. However, I know many of the exact opposite opinion.

The other development was a hardening of issues in experimental writing. I have been much involved in the development of feminist writing, and the gradual recognition, even in the mainstream, of inclusive language issues. The book, *Reflecting Praise*, was published in 1993, halfway through the World Council of Churches' Decade for the Churches in Solidarity with Women (1988–98), by Stainer & Bell and Women in Theology. This joint venture includes texts by June Boyce Tillman, Judith Driver and many other women writers.

Male writers are also represented, including Sydney Carter and Brian Wren. Brian Wren's important book, *What Language Shall I Borrow?* is a long, consistent look at the issues of inclusive language.[14] The experience of writers in this field raises a number of issues.

First, all human beings are not men or brothers. All my years of growing up in the Church were marked by singing hymns about men. The grammatical tenet, that the male (rather coyly) embraces the female, is not appropriate to language in the present day and, I believe, hid a latent sexism even when it was applicable grammatically. Now we sing of sisters and brothers, women and men.

And there are sisters and women whose stories are being

rediscovered in song. Women from scripture – Miriam, dancing on the threshold of the Red Sea, Deborah leading the people of Israel through difficult times, Sarah, Rachel, Rebecca, the many anonymous women who met Jesus, commemorated in Brian Wren's hymn 'Woman in the night', Mary the mother of Jesus as a real woman, Mary Magdalene and so on. There are great stories from the Christian tradition: Hildegard, Hilda, Julian, as well as Josephine Butler and Elizabeth Fry from our own time. These are recalled in song.

Elizabeth Cosnett's hymn, 'For God's sake let us dare' invites worshippers to 'pray like Josephine'. The Josephine to which it refers is Josephine Butler, social reformer in the field of prostitution, whose political views sprang from her deep prayer life. The hymn follows Josephine in denouncing the double standard still evident in views on prostitution, and the underlying issues of degradation.

And what of God? Hymns which refer to God in feminine terms are explosive in the extreme. People who are happy to sing of God as an inanimate object like a rock, or an animal like a lion, will not sing about God as a mother.

Three hymns provide samples of possible approaches to singing of God as female. Some of these are simply joyous expressions of experience, such as Judith Driver's 'My God is woman'. Others, such as my own 'Dear mother God' are explicitly based on scripture, in this instance, Deuteronomy 32.11, in which God speaks through Moses of Godself as a mother bird teaching the chicks to fly and Isaiah 40.31, where the strong mount up on eagles' wings. Yet others, such as Betty Wendelborn's 'My mother Jesus', based on the words of Julian of Norwich, honour a long tradition of seeing the Persons of the Trinity in female form. But there is something visceral in people's response, which even reference to scripture or tradition will not allay.

This is a lovely field to be working in. The life of women and men springs from the pages of scripture and history. We just haven't sung about them before! For many people, the discovery of female language about God is entirely liberating, and goes with non-hierarchical, non-triumphalist theologies.

It is not just about inclusive language. Feminist theology is only one aspect of a wider change in theological thinking. Perhaps the clearest and best-known exponent of the new theologies in Britain is the Iona Community. Using traditional Scottish tunes as well as newly composed music, the writers of the Iona Community address issues of inclusivity, homelessness, mingling the holy with ordinary life. These have been taken up very widely, and found a ready and popular acceptance in congregations and hymn books.

One example of the work of this prolific group of writers is 'Will you come and follow me', sung to the tune 'Kelvingrove'. This lures the singer into its very challenging words: 'Will you kiss the leper clean, and do such as this unseen?' 'Will you love the you you hide?' A second, 'Enemy of apathy', refers to the Spirit of God as female – 'She sits like a bird, brooding on the waters.' This is slightly less controversial, since the Hebrew for Spirit is feminine anyway, but this hymn still raises hackles.

Now, again, experimental and traditional hymnody is coming together in new publications, such as the Scottish book, *Common Ground* (1998), which includes a great deal of the Iona writing.

The future

I began by saying that talk of a future for hymns may be optimistic. However, the field is still very much alive. The great English hymn writers of the last 50 years, Brian Wren, Fred Pratt Green, Alan Gaunt, Timothy Dudley Smith and Fred Kaan, have handed on a tradition of well-written, thoughtful and courageous texts, which are still graspable by a congregation in worship. Iona has given us a whole style and language of hymnody, which is full of life and creativity.

As well as handing on a tradition, one hymn writer has made a more tangible contribution to the future. Fred Pratt Green, one of the greatest writers of our age, set up a trust to encourage new writing, based on his own considerable royalties. The trust has supported projects by individual writers and groups of writers. With the fall of the Berlin Wall, the trust responded to some emerging traditions from Central and Eastern Europe. Latterly, it has established a CD resource, *HymnQuest*, an interactive database compiled by Fred Pratt Green which enables worship leaders to search a huge number of hymn texts and tunes, and actively encourages the discovery of new material.

As editor of *Worship Live*, a worship journal published three times a year by Stainer & Bell, I am constantly delighted by the amount and quality of writing. New writers appear all the time, and some of the writers who were new when we started five years ago, are now becoming established. The writing is fun, images are fresh and new, the texts pull no punches and continue to challenge, and, above all, they engage both heart and mind. *Worship Live* is but one among a great number of published and electronic resources for new writing.

The millennium has spawned a number of initiatives in hymnody, suggesting that there is still popular life in this medium. The millennium hymn competition run by Canon Michael Saward of St Paul's Cathedral attracted 750 entries.

The book *Songs for the New Millennium* has nearly 200 texts and considered many, many more.[15] Its stated aim is 'to bring together real worship that expresses the breadth of the human experience of God, from tears to laughter, from doubt to enthusiastic faith; diverse worship that draws on the riches of the widest possible cross-section of the Christian faith community; creative worship that allows music and poetry to play a central role'.

In October 2000, the Methodist Church Music Society and Fred Pratt Green Trust held a conference on 'Singing in the New Millennium' at which some twenty writers and composers spoke and led workshops. Three 'prophets' looked forward to the future of hymnody before an audience of several hundred practitioners.

Where is all this new writing coming from?

There is, as in previous generations, a wonderful cross-fertilization from other than English writing. As in Catherine Winkworth's day, we are benefiting from European traditions. Europe is developing new identities following the collapse of the Soviet Union. Organizations such as the Conference of European Churches (CEC) and the Ecumenical Forum of European Christian Women (EFECW) are vastly enriched by the presence of previously excluded nations, and – of course – by their hymn traditions.

Many authors and composers are finding inspiration in writing for ecumenical conferences. Claudia Mitscha Eibl's humorous and challenging texts livened recent women's conferences. Written in German, they are translated into French and English, though concepts such as *Rabensmutter* – the reviled mother who wants to enjoy life as well as having children – do not translate well. Per Harling, a Swedish writer, has written a good deal of material for this field, and is becoming widely known and sung.

Through greater global communication, and through the cultural diversity of our own islands, we are able to draw on African, Caribbean, Asian and other traditions. The Baptist World Alliance book, *World Praise* (1995) has brought a number of texts and tunes into popular use. The book is the very deliberate result of a Baptist World Alliance Worship Commission set up in 1990 'to seek means of worship appropriate for our generation'.

The Iona Community has been instrumental in bringing a variety of world music into general church worship. John Bell's facility in standing before a congregation of thousands or a group of a dozen, and simply leading singing, has made new material accessible. Congregations, who would never have imagined that they could move beyond tunes, or at least types of tunes, that they knew, find themselves singing, unaccompanied, part-songs and music from Latin America, Africa, and a whole range of sources. John Bell will argue that it is time to gather world music in a systematic way, as writers like Catherine Winkworth gathered German lyrics.

In the meantime, writers such as Shirley Murray in New Zealand, writing in English but celebrating a Pacific culture, challenge our cultural imperialism with songs like, 'Upside down Christmas'. *Alleluia Aotearoa* (1993), from the New Zealand Hymnbook Trust, offers a consciously Pacific book. There are texts in Polynesian languages, and the bi-cultural perspective of New Zealand is celebrated in songs like, 'Colour me free', which has become immensely popular in my own multicultural congregation.

Sadly, this kind of new writing is by no means global. I recently joined a huge Chinese congregation just outside Shanghai, and recognized every hymn. Though the singing was in Chinese, I could join in without difficulty in 'Trust and obey', 'What a friend we have in Jesus' and other similar hymns set to the English tunes. In China and in Korea, I have asked for copies of newly published hymn books, and asked who are the writers of new material, to be told that the only current activity is translating American or English charismatic texts. In Guyana, I sang from *Congregational Praise*, a book from which – good as it undoubtedly was for its own generation – many congregational churches in Britain have moved on.

In Britain and America, much new writing deals with challenging social areas. This is aided by the development of a whole series of 'Special Sundays' on themes such as homelessness and unemployment, and days such as AIDS day. New material is also bringing a different focus to the traditional 'alternative Christian year' in writing for seasons like Harvest and Remembrance. Other material is inspired by the publication of new lectionaries, and focuses on the liturgical year.

The Decade for the Churches in Solidarity with Women gave a tremendous boost to general feminist and inclusive writing of the kind mentioned in the previous section, but it also raised the issue of violence and abuse. Recent resources have included hymns, sometimes solo songs with a congregational chorus, which help break the silence in this sensitive area. Linda Shepherd's 'Called to make justice', with its brutal first lines, 'There's a woman who is crying as the blows begin to fall,/ There's a child who is screaming as he's thrown against the wall', is one of these.

Here, again, the picture is not of unbroken success for hymn writing. The attitudes that I mentioned at the beginning of the chapter are current. Congregations who like modern music for worship are largely not singing hymns, even good, modern hymns. And congregations who like a traditional style of music have no access to modern writing in the idiom.

The Iona community has a vital part to play in this scenario. By writing and introducing fresh new hymns set to folk or folk-style tunes, they have opened the way for the acceptance of current hymn writing. They have been aided by the popularity of Celtic spirituality, and by their grounding in a strong and attractive community.

If there is a future for hymnody as an art form and a productive form for Christian worship, it will owe a great deal to Iona for breaking down some of the barriers between traditional and modern music and words. It is in hymn writing, as a form in which a congregation, singing together, can explore sometimes very radical ideas in an equalizing form of worship, that Christian worship can grapple with its witness to the postmodern world in which we live.

We are no longer in a post-war world, struggling to make sense of Auschwitz and Hiroshima. This is the world of the Internet, globalization, issues of equality and marginalization. A postmodern world no longer seeks answers in the 'big picture'. Diversity of lifestyle clashes with attempts to return to forms of moral control. Christians struggle or leap to find God's purpose in a new age and, of necessity, they come to many different conclusions. Christianity lives alongside other major faiths, exploratory spiritualities and a secular concern with great issues of justice and moral living. The hymn writers of the third millennium will need to engage congregations with this whole range of life-issues. Controversy will not fade from the Christian arena, nor from its music.

Is there a Future for the Church Musician?

JOHN FERGUSON

I s there a future for the church musician? Rather than marshal an array of statistics, studies of trends or collection of quotes from the many articles and books which might inform (at least tangentially) any response to this question, I wish to answer this question in a more personal way. My reading and reflection upon the issues facing church music-makers, be they composers, choir directors, organists or praise band leaders has been leavened by conversations and experience with people making church music, people who care about what they are doing, people who worry about the future not just of the professional church musician but of the role of music in the life of the Church. In a sense, one could say that what follows is a kind of personal credo, a statement affirming the inherent integrity and necessity of what the church musician does. This credo reflects my conviction that the role of music in the life of the Church is a vital one and that those who lead music are and will be needed, provided they understand clearly what it is they are to lead.

God created us to sing

I believe that God made music, created things so that music is possible, designed us so that we are able to sing. God arranged the world with music as a physical possibility and equipped us with ears that could discern a much wider range of frequencies than that required to hear speech. When the morning stars sang at creation a precedent was established. When we feel strongly about things we sing – from the lullaby of a mother to her child to the lament over the loss of a child. From the song of lament transformed into hope of Psalm 130 to the joy of Psalm 150, we, God's children, sing. Miriam sang, Mary sang, David sang, Simeon sang. The Bible is filled with singing, as is all of nature around us.

What is it about singing, a few pitches ordered in time, that has such evocative power? What is it about the sounds of singing, the colours of instruments, that enable us to praise, that assist us better to understand the God whom we praise? Music is an expressive language with the potential to strengthen and deepen the impact of words. The changing colour, texture and character of music have extraordinary ability to communicate. Perhaps this interpretive power of music explains why Christians have always felt a need to sing their faith. The great, good news of the gospel is too much for mere words; it needs music with its wide range of moods and styles to tell the story of God's creating and redeeming acts. Thus the primary role of music in worship is to be an exegetical servant to the singing of the Word. Of course, much that is sung is not specifically biblical, yet at an elemental level, most music sung at worship reflects an encounter with that Word. When Christians gather, they sing their story, they sing their faith, they sing God's Word as they sing praise and prayer to the Lord. In the process they remind themselves and each other who they are as God's people. They celebrate the great gifts God has given them, and in the process employ one of those gifts, music.

When Christians gather for worship and sing, and make together in community joyful noise to the Lord, they are being profoundly countercultural. For many today it is not 'cool' to make music, and our spectator mentality encourages us to watch others make music instead of doing it ourselves whether it be in church or the concert hall. Our challenge as church musicians is to encourage this countercultural behaviour of our congregations, to encourage the song of the congregation, the assembled gathering of believers. Our call is to teach, enable, nurture, enrich and inspire that song. Our challenge is to be tenacious in holding on to the notion that all God's children still have a place in the choir because God invented the choir in the first place.

What song do we sing?

What song should we sing when we gather as Christians? This dimension of the larger question of the future of the Church's song has at least two facets. First, we must sing as a congregation, not as performers for a congregation. Second, we must sing music that is viable, accessible for congregational song.

I believe that our American church music practice has suffered from a confusion of purposes and understandings. Most church musicians (especially the full-time professionals) think of themselves as conductors and/or organ performers. For the conductors, the organized choirs of the churches they serve are perceived as their chief responsibility. For the organist, the preparation of the voluntaries, the preludes, offertories and postludes is considered primary. Certainly this is the case if one examines the emphasis experienced while in training to be a church musician. Yet the preparation and performance of voluntaries and anthems, while worthwhile and significant, is not the central mission of the church musician. Our confusion of purpose is based in part on our training and experience. It is based in part on the history of the development of the profession in this country.

In America, the concept of organized, rehearsed church choirs is relatively new. In the late nineteenth century, most churches, especially those with 'good' music programmes, had a paid, professional quartet. Early in the twentieth century, choirs became more common, partly as an outgrowth of the St Olaf College and Westminster Choir College traditions. The 'cradle to the grave' choir programme, now beginning to lose its vitality in some churches, became the norm only after the Second World War, especially in the large congregations of the growing suburbs filled with children of the post-war baby boom. The strongest choirs and music programmes evolved in the mainline denominations where greater financial resources for professional leadership were available, sometimes including paid choir singers.

When possible and especially where an adult choir is available, the church musicians serving these large, mainline churches tend to select repertoire from the European choral tradition, repertoire almost exclusively conceived for the professional church music establishments in the great churches of Europe. In selecting and performing this repertoire, many have never considered the irony that the European church music practice and repertoire we know about and wish to emulate is what could be called 'cathedral practice', an approach to worship never envisioned for and infrequently practised in the local parish churches of Europe of yesterday and especially of today. In the great churches, especially the English cathedral and collegiate chapels, music is generally (and increasingly) made in a very different way from the way it is made in the parish churches. Most American church musicians never read about or experience music in the European parish churches. We know about, hear recordings from, and visit the cathedrals and collegiate chapels. Then we try to make cathedral music in our parish churches, overlooking the primary choir, which is the gathered assembly. In a similar way, organists tend to focus on the voluntaries instead of the creative leadership of the gathered assembly.

But the discussion of music practice, in which American amateurs perform art music conceived for European professionals, ignores the more basic question that still confuses us today. What is church music? Is it different from sacred music? I consider sacred music to be music inspired by religious ideas and/or texts. It may find its place in worship, usually as attendant music, enriching the experience of worship for many. It may find its place in a church choir concert, organ recital or programme given by an orchestra and chorus. Church music is music that directly enables the worshipper to encounter and address God through active participation. It includes the hymns and other liturgical music that serve as basic parts of the structure of the service. Of course these distinctions are not ironclad and sometimes the same piece of music can function in both categories. Bach's church cantatas were conceived as church music, but in America today they almost always function as sacred music.

Unfortunately most church music curricula tend to focus primarily upon training people to conduct and perform sacred music. Most students of church music spend little time considering the primary responsibility of the church musician, which is to nurture the congregation's song, not to perform sacred music, which though it adorns the worship life of the Church is not essential to it. Thus, when faced with challenges and doubts as we are today, the person trained as a performer of sacred music may be poorly equipped to respond to questions about styles and the role of church music – questions which are as much theological as musical.

Then what song does the congregation sing? I believe it is folk song, traditional song, the people's song. Church music as defined above is primarily the song of the assembly. As the song of the people it must be both accessible and durable. It must be capable of expressing a wide spectrum of ideas encompassing the entire range of human emotions. No single, specific 'style' of congregational music can achieve this other than the traditional music of all nationalities and cultures. Art music (sometimes called classical music) is wonderfully rich in styles capable of expressing the widest range of emotions and

ideas, but with few exceptions it is too difficult for congregational participation. Conversely, most contemporary pop
music is aesthetically too shallow to be an adequate vehicle for
the entire story God's people need to sing. In addition, most
pop music is like art music in that it is too difficult for congregational use. It is music for performers, music to be heard,
not sung by congregations. As John Bell reminds us,

> It is notable that some of those who, in a previous era, were
> keen to dispense the tyranny of the organist and choir
> because they did not let the people sing, are now fulfilling
> the arrogant and elitist roles they previously denounced, as
> the worship of God's people becomes dominated by
> amplification which highlights the performer's skills, and
> overhead projectors which forbid any deep engagement
> with the text being sung.[2]

In contrast, folk music coming from the people is ideal for
group singing. Traditional hymnody should be included in
this category of song. Its texts and tunes (the good ones) have
endured the test of time and continue to speak with integrity,
relevance and power.[3] Hymns and their tunes can be passed
on orally just as other folk song because they are a type of folk
music. It is this rich treasure of song that must be a primary
concern of the church musician. It is this rich heritage which
must be shared, nurtured, explored and expanded.

For whom do we sing?

This question is especially timely today when many worship
leaders seem to overlook the fundamental reason for worship.
In their genuine concern for the proclamation of the good
news of the gospel, they ignore the theological imperative
that worship is not for the people, but is the people's gift to
God. Worship leaders are not the performers; they are the
prompters. The gathered congregation is the performing

group, joining the saints of all time and beyond time in giving praise, making melody to the Lord. Worship is a performance, an offering directed towards God. Church music is a part of that offering of all the people gathered before the throne of the Lord most high. When one considers worship in this basic way, some of the present tensions surrounding styles of worship begin to pale before the central issue – are we at worship?

Lutheran liturgical theologian Marva Dawn has argued:

When we agree that God must be the subject and object of our worship, we discover that the bitter war between 'traditional' and 'contemporary' styles misses the real issue. Both can easily become idolatrous. Many defenders of traditional worship pridefully insist that the historic liturgy of the Church is the only way to do it right, while their counterparts advocating contemporary worship styles often try to control God and convert people by their own efforts. Neither pride nor presumption can inhabit praise; both prevent God from being the subject and object of worship.[4]

The above quotation needs no preparation, no setting of context for anyone at work today as a worship leader. The tensions surrounding the issue of how we worship and what music we will use for worship have led to much pain and anguish for both musician and clergy. The lover of 'traditional' church music is accused of being insensitive to the needs of the worshippers being served. Often the classically trained church musician is accused of having no interest in evangelism, no concern for the many who have yet to hear the good news of the gospel. Such accusations may be accurate in a few instances, but my experience suggests that most church musicians care deeply about the spiritual welfare of those they serve and are as anxious as their clergy colleagues to reach out to those who have yet to hear of God's loving concern for all creation.

Meanwhile the words entertainment and evangelism have been coupled together and in the process entertainment as 'worship' has become a virtue. In a recent article, Peter Gomes, minister of the Memorial Church at Harvard University, Cambridge, Massachusetts, describes the interesting phenomenon of tour groups from overseas paying to visit and observe worship at some of the major African-American congregations in Harlem in New York City. The visitors sit in the balcony and watch what is happening down below. Members and clergy of the churches being visited are beginning to wonder about what is happening. In becoming tourist attractions, are they in danger of losing the integrity of their worship? If people pay to watch it, has worship become mere entertainment? Gomes then goes on to relate his experience attending an evensong service at King's College, Cambridge, England. 'On my first visit to King's many years ago, I was astonished to read the neatly lettered signs in the pews inviting the congregation not to join in singing.'[5]

While the style is radically different, is evensong as spectator sport in King's any different from the service in Harlem? Are these experiences worship or entertainment? For most of the 'performers' in each instance, we can hope that it is worship. For those attending, or those just watching, it is more likely that it is entertainment, spectacle. In this context is there any difference between featuring a large, spectacular pipe organ as a device to attract people and featuring an excellent 'worship band' as an attraction? While one might argue about the styles of music appropriate for these radically different musical media and the subliminal messages these different musical styles may send, using either solely as devices to attract people is a manipulative, marketing device. A concert performance of the *Saint Matthew Passion*, considered an outreach activity by a large, mainline Protestant church, is as much entertainment evangelism as a concert by a performer of contemporary Christian music at a Baptist church. Based upon the definitions proposed earlier, both feature sacred music, but neither is church music. Both invite us to listen; both have the potential to inspire us, to move us, perhaps to help us better to encounter God. But both encourage us to be passive, not active; to be spectators, not participants in the worship of God. Is this wrong? No. Is there a place in the Church when the performance of sacred music, even the offering of a service more as 'spectator sport' can be considered legitimate? Of course. The point is not that such activity is wrong but that it must not distract church musicians from their normative vocation – the leadership of the entire congregation in making joyful noise to the Lord.

If there is a future for the church musician, especially the professionally trained, full-time or part-time church musician, it is more likely to be in the historic, biblical model of the cantor who leads the song of the assembly. Of course a portion of that leadership role also involves nurturing the subsets of the large, congregational choir. These subsets – the organized, rehearsed choirs – are a vital part of the overall scheme of things.

Lest I be misunderstood, I have nothing against church choirs. In every church I have served I have been blessed with wonderful, talented people who worked hard with me to be as fine a choral ensemble as humanly possible. We have sung everything from Bach and Tallis to Britten and Distler. Today I have the privilege of working with a superb college choir and know that upon graduation, many of my singers hope to find a good church choir where they may continue to make joyful choral noise to the Lord. Yet in my travels about the United States, I find that in many places we are not working hard enough to nurture our church choirs. Many directors seem afraid to challenge their singers, worrying that if they are too demanding they will lose them. Yet these volunteers, all with many options for use of their free time, choose to be a part of a church choir. They seem to understand, sometimes better than their directors, that their responsibility is both to sing with and to lead the congregation, as well as to sing what the congregation cannot sing. They come to rehearsal seeking a realistic challenge. They like to sing music of quality and want to do it well. Certainly the recent growth of the community chorus movement in the United States, which involves both adult and children's choirs, has been encouraged in part because of the decline in quality of our church choirs. We seem to be afraid to challenge our people, in this case our choral singers. So the best singers are looking elsewhere for opportunities to sing challenging literature.

So I am not at all against Byrd, Brahms or Britten being sung at worship. But I am concerned that the balance between the work of the primary choir, the congregation, and the other choirs in any parish needs to be readjusted. The organized choir needs to serve as a provider of beautiful music and as a training ground for the song of the assembly. By its example, by the care with which it sings the liturgy and hymns, it becomes a role model for the primary choir, the entire congregation.

A particularly potent way that the organized choir can serve the entire body of believers is through singing anthems based upon hymns. There are many fine hymn anthems in the repertoire. In a sense, many of J. S. Bach's chorale-based cantata movements are prototypes of this genre of choral song. The hymn anthems of Charles V. Stanford, especially his beautiful setting of 'O for a closer walk with God' (to the tune 'Caithness' from the Scottish Psalter), are more recent and realistic prototypes. In America another kind of hymn anthem envisioning congregational participation has evolved, often called the 'hymn concertato'. Ralph Vaughan Williams' arrangements of 'All hail the power of Jesus' name' ('Miles Lane') and 'The old hundredth psalm tune' are marvellous examples of this genre. My concertato on 'The king of love my shepherd is' is typical of the many being produced in

America in that it has stanzas for all to sing, stanzas for all women, all men and two for solo choir.[6] In the solo choir stanzas I try to treat text and tune more rhapsodically and with exegetical text-painting since the absence of congregation allows for greater compositional freedom. Of course each stanza has a unique accompaniment, which further contributes to the unpacking of the concepts presented in the text. Such concertatos can provide musical challenges for the choir and invite the congregation into a more intense encounter with text and tune.[7]

So there are many ways in which the choir can be an encourager of congregational song. Through the theological, vocal and musical education, which must be a part of all choir rehearsals, especially those of the youth and children's choirs, the organized choir becomes the experiential leaven in the loaf for the song of the entire assembly.

What about the organist?

Where do the organ and the organist fit into my vision for the future of music in the Church? In spite of the many congregations with a praise team or worship band, in most mainline churches in America the organ and organist remain the primary instrumental leader and accompanist of congregational song. No single instrument played by one person is as well-equipped to energize a wide variety of styles of song as the organ, provided it is used well. The organ can undergird and support a congregation better than any other single instrument. It can project the melody as well or better than any solo instrument while offering a wide range of colours and textures which can be used to exegete the spirit of text and tune, and to respond to it. Of course a fine orchestra or concert band can lead singing and a 'worship band' is capable of leading a more limited range of musical styles. The disadvantage of these options is that to succeed they require a group of talented musicians willing to rehearse regularly, a group that understands how to lead congregational song. In addition there are few good arrangements available for these ensembles that are also appropriate to energize and exegete the texts of the wide variety of songs required for a rich repertoire of congregational song. Here is where the colour and scope of the organ becomes so significant, provided the organist has been trained as a song leader and can spend the requisite practice time in weekly preparation so that the song of the assembly is led with creativity and theological sensitivity. Unfortunately these skills have been ignored in most traditional curricula for organ study. If the organ is to survive as a valued servant of the Church and leader of the congregation's song, much more attention must be given to the exploration of its great potential for leading group song.

As we explore the organ's enormous resources as leader of congregational song, we will need to address the question of how to use these resources. Leadership by sonic assault is not the answer. The organist must know when to lead, when to accompany and when to let go, allowing the people to sing unaccompanied. Song leading from the organ does not mean total control of the singing by the organist. Rather, it involves inviting the people – encouraging and exciting them – into song. It also means affirming an approach to organ building that produces instruments whose ensemble sound encourages others to join with it in making music. The ensemble sound must not be too dense or opaque, and always it must sing. The organ must also be flexible and easy to use so that the great varieties of sounds inherent in a fine instrument are quickly available.

Is there a future for the church musician? Yes, provided we continue to rethink our reason for being and focus upon our call to service as church musicians. The following job description is offered as another way to articulate how I envision church music as a part of the life of the typical American congregation of today and in the immediate future.

Job Description for Music Director and Organist
St Swithen's in the Swamp Presbylutheristopal Church

The people of St Swithen's consider gathering for the worship of Almighty God as the primary reason for their congregation's existence and in this context seek a person of faith to become a part of their worshipping community of believers. The responsibilities of music director and organist are difficult to articulate completely or precisely, but the following job description provides an overview of what we believe to be the primary responsibilities of those called to lead our worship through music.

I. Teach singing

A. Enable the song of the primary choir of St Swithen's, the gathered congregation, each Lord's Day. That leadership shall come primarily but not exclusively from the sounds of the organ and choirs as they lead us in our song.

B. Conduct the Adult Choir and supervise the directors of the younger choirs. This assignment includes the preparation of the choirs to lead the song of the congregation through the regular rehearsal of service music and hymnody as well as the preparation of examples of the best of choral literature appropriate for each ensemble to be offered as music to enrich worship.

C. Encourage a growth in appreciation of the historic song of our worshipping tradition while being sensitive to the many ways that the song of the redeemed has been sung, both today and over the centuries.

D. Expand the ways our song is sung through the introduction and utilization of a wide range of instruments and instrumentalists to assist in leading our song.

II. Be liturgist in residence

A. Work with the clergy and Worship Committee in the planning and preparation of worship.

B. Design musical materials to support and enrich the worship of this congregation (compose, arrange, and encourage the composition of music and/or find music in published sources as appropriate).

C. Be creative in the integration of the themes of the liturgical seasons and appointed scriptural readings into the selection of music for worship. Lead and present that music in ways that bring text and tune alive.

III. Be diligent in practice and study in order to lead the music with creativity as well as technical excellence

IV. Serve as resource person to the congregation

A. Oversee the maintenance of the musical instruments of the congregation, including proposing options to improve and broaden that collection of resources.

B. Assist the Environment Committee in its work of preparing the sanctuary for worship in ways that reflect the varying themes and foci of the church calendar.

While others could add to and expand this description, it does focus upon the essential concerns which we, as church musicians must address as we serve our congregations.

Is there a future for us church musicians? Yes, but that future might not be like the past many of us have known. How will things be different? No one can say for sure. How we make and lead church music will and should change, but as long as we continue to work to lead and enrich the congregation's song there will be a future for us.

There will be church music as long as God's people gather for worship. There must be. God designed it that way.

11

Renewing the Past in the Present:
The Living Art of Church Music

JOHN HARPER

Throughout this chapter my principal point of reference is
the Church of England, not to be narrow and parochial,
but to give focus; and therefore when I talk of Christian worship it is a worship based on formal orders and established
liturgical texts.

In the continuing processes of liturgical formation and
liturgical change there is counterpoint between the evaluation
of a received past, the review of present practice, and the
shaping of future use. Within that wider context music exists
both as a constituent element and as a means of approaching
the whole of worship. As the Church of England begins to
publish its new orders of worship, *Common Worship*,[1] the challenge to composers is particularly great and difficult. It is great
because of the scope and choices of the new forms of service;
it is difficult because of the fragmentation of styles of worship
and music for worship, and the reduction in the number of
suitably skilled musical personnel to facilitate music in worship. In writing here, I draw on a variety of experiences as a
liturgical musician, mostly during that period of liturgical
ferment between 1960 and 2000: as a choral director who has
composed for the choirs he has directed within the liturgy; as
a scholar keen to understand the heritage and history of the
Western liturgy and its music;[2] and now as someone respons-

ible for initiatives in the training, education and formation of musicians working in the service of the Church. But the central issue of this chapter is the composer, and specifically the location of the composer in relation to the phenomenon of worship.

Within a more general context there are two specific and datable projects related to the year 2000. The first is the commission from the Cathedral Organists' Association to Professor Nigel Osborne for a new setting of the canticles. The second is my own involvement in the preparation of music for *Common Worship*.

Worship as listening to the total music

All worship exists within time. The shaping of sound within time is at the heart of all music. The shaping of prayer and praise within time is the essence of all worship. No matter what the content or context, no matter how many items, how many participants in a formal act of worship, it requires co-herence, shape, balance, moments of climax and tension, moments of repose. Formal worship is of its nature close to music. At its best it resonates with and echoes the divine.

Every act of worship is an act of collective composition in which a series of events, some musical, some spoken, some accompanied by gesture and movement, some dependent on silence and stillness occur within a time frame marked by coming in and going out. In fact many services are routine and the shaping of time in this way is either fortuitous or dependent on a team used to working together.

Christian worship can be regarded as a musical mosaic, in which the total experience far transcends the dazzling intellect of the sermon, the cadences of the readings, the polished performance of a choir, the flowing movements of the cere-monial or the still silence of a period of prayer. In fact where prayer and praise are offered in truth and sincerity the divine music may be perceived in spite of a naive sermon, poor reading, grim singing, gauche movement, because there is a powerful commitment to prayer. As his father reminded the American composer Charles Ives: 'Don't mistake the sound for the music!'[3]

Where beautiful choral worship seems arid, it may be that we have lost sight of the shaping of time; that we have stopped listening to the total music. Where there is a group of people whose primary objective is to share in prayer through music, there is a need to stand back; to ask questions about the coherence, shape and balance of worship. Worship, and at that musical worship, does not depend on music. It does require silence in order to value the sounds; it requires stillness in order to value the movement.

How then does a composer set about writing music for Christian worship? In what ways is the process distinct from any other kind of composition? Identity, boundaries and control are key issues. Most often a composer making a piece defines these features: the new work is an extension of that person. The composer owns the work, shapes it, wishes it to stand on its own merits. It is almost the reverse when writing liturgical music. Music for worship has to be part of a larger and collective identity; it is bounded by the larger context of the liturgy; controlled in scale and ethos to contribute to the larger music of worship. The composer is challenged to demonstrate strength and purpose in the new work, and yet has to contain that strength within the overall context of worship.

The formation of clergy and church musicians for worship

Composers can be inhibited by this constrained challenge, especially in responding to commissions. Remarkably few of the carols commissioned each year for the King's College, Cambridge, Christmas Eve Carol Service have become established in the repertory. Both of the new works written for the National Millennium Service at St Paul's Cathedral seemed to be clothed in unease. The technical constraints of the choral resource, limitations of rehearsal, and the platform of worship may be disincentives. Anglican church choirs are trained in a post-monastic tradition to be neutral and undemonstrative – a smile is quite unacceptable; their uniformity in robes represents the suppression of the individual in a collective act of music-making and worship. Some of them rehearse for fewer hours than they perform. These are not the musical forces to attract the adventurous composer. Nor is the circumstance particularly inviting. Church music is heard at uncivilized hours when most of the world is going home for tea, or on the one day in the week when the whole family is free to go out together.

Not surprisingly, perhaps, few composers of distinction have been attracted to write practical music for Anglican liturgy. When one compares this with the engagement and imagination composers demonstrate in the world of educational and community music, this is quite a surprise. Perhaps the Church has failed to make the connection with them, failed to communicate the creative opportunity.

I am currently engaged in managing a commission from the Cathedral Organists' Association (COA) for new evening canticles. The COA went to Nigel Osborne, one of the bright young British moderns of the 1970s, skilled in writing advanced music for voices. Far more central to the commission was his interest and experience in community music, and his humanitarian concern demonstrated in the creative work he has undertaken over recent years in Croatia, Bosnia and Kosovo.

The boundaries set at the COA's behest were specific and not especially attractive: a concise setting for everyday use, no more than twenty minutes' rehearsal time after first learning, limitations on vocal range, music to be usable by choirs with professional men as well as those with untrained volunteers.

Nigel Osborne's response has been imaginative and generous: he is writing morning as well as evening canticles because the challenge inspired him. He is writing settings suitable not just for cathedral choir but which can be sung with a congregation or by unison voices alone. With genuine humility a composer of his experience has offered the drafts for comment and review. He is very conscious of the continuity of tradition: his predecessor as Reid Professor at Edinburgh was Kenneth Leighton, whose Second Service was also a commission from the COA. There is both collectivity and continuity in Osborne's Millennium Canticles: 'I'm long past my narcissistic phase as a composer . . . It's good when music is being used and heard.'[4]

These, it seems to me, are the creative relations we need to foster. But such fostering is just one part of a broader and extended process of formation of clergy and church musicians, a process of reaffirming the nature and function of worship, of re-establishing the meaning and purpose of music in worship. Few church musicians have an adequate training in liturgy, theology and the theology of music. Few Anglican clergy have more than a couple of hours of practical training in music for liturgy during their years at theological college, let alone any more profound engagement in the subject. Where liturgical music blossoms it is most often the result of luck and good personal relations. Where it is not working, clergy are often thrashing about for solutions with good intentions but inadequate knowledge or experience. In those circumstances it is tempting to settle for a quick fix based on the lowest common denominator, or else to give up.

This is perhaps my greatest challenge at the Royal School of Church Music (RSCM), to work with the Church and with cognate organizations, to develop a programme of education, training and qualifications which is rooted in understanding worship and music in worship, and not based exclusively on developing musical skills. Programmes for educating church musicians, and the expectation of engaging and paying a professionally trained church musician, are well-established in Germany, Scandinavia and USA. But in Britain, where the tradition is so well-established, this is largely alien. It may be necessary to accept that we have to take our fingers out of the dyke in the short term if we are to build secure foundations for church music in twenty years time. Without a trained body of musicians and an informed body of clergy the long-term future can only be bleak. Already at the RSCM there is a preliminary strategy directed towards 2020, with an aim to have 2,000 trained liturgical musicians in Britain, and a better-informed clergy and laity. The programme of education, training and qualifications is in an advanced stage of preparation.[5] What has to be built over that time is a culture of engaging church musicians, perhaps as part of a portfolio of employment,[6] and where a group of churches (perhaps not even of the same denomination) might 'share' the services of a trained liturgical musician to animate and guide groups of amateurs and volunteers. And their musical skills and liturgical understanding will need to be both broad and flexible at a time when local diversity is such a strong feature even of the worship of a single denomination. The days of standard provision (small choir, organ, standard psalter and hymnbook) are gone; the more realistic model for the Church will be that of the school or creative arts workshop where the manifestation of the music is determined by the skills, resources and interests of the group creating it.

Fostering music in centres of excellence, and in small parish churches

The present lack of a framework for liturgical or musical formation, training and education in the Church of England is only one aspect of the fragility of church music, and especially cathedral music. In spite of the international recognition of its uniqueness and worth, the survival of English cathedral music has depended on a mere thread of continuity over the past 450 years. It still relies on a handful of properly endowed choral foundations, and thereafter on the goodwill and enthusiasm of able students, amateur volunteers, keen children and their families. The standards achieved in choral foundations are perhaps higher than ever, but there are ominous signs of stress. The cathedrals recognize the problems of recruiting children and adult singers in new social circumstances, the demands of sustaining an expanding programme of services, concerts and tours in a changed cultural environment, and the need for extensive endowment. Those who work in church music in a wider sphere are all too aware of the rapidity of change in resource and circumstance. We may speak of composing music for Christian worship in the third millennium, but we may find that there is a continuing and rapid shrinkage of musicians for whom to compose.

Part of the problem lies in the dissipation of the financial resource. Something in excess of £8 million is spent on the provision of choral foundations in Britain each year, over half on scholarships and other educational support for children. Although a substantial sum, it is spread over more than 60 cathedrals and colleges. With a shortage of children and adults there is the inevitable logic that the resource must be focused on a smaller number of well-funded, well-resourced centres of excellence,[7] and that other institutions will need to find other kinds of solution. Centres of excellence need also to be centres of creativity, development and training. They must be linked to other more modest foundations and to the networks of parish music. The old 'minster' model may be useful at a number of levels in church music, just as it is proving to be in the clerical staffing of parishes.

The trend towards choral foundations as training grounds is already there. Indeed, some of the most highly regarded choral foundations are centres of training, based in educational rather than cathedral foundations, and relying on a relatively in-experienced and rapidly changing body of undergraduate or recent graduates as 'adult' singers. The enthusiasm and the relative instability of such a choral group are elements which contribute to its vitality and quality, guided by musicians of the highest calibre. These young choirs can be nurtured and developed, but there is no career progression within the Church once they leave: increasingly, young singers and organists leave university with their sights set on a freelance career in the secular musical world. Structures need to be put into place, and strategies developed. And composers need to be included in the planning of those structures and strategies.

That, of course, presumes that composers are writing for choirs and musicians. The trends in pastoral liturgy emphasize the ownership and involvement in worship of the whole assembly. The choir or the music group is just one part of that assembly, and not necessarily a dominant part. What of music composed for the people?

Historically, there has been very little liturgical music for the people in the Church of England. The *Book of Common Prayer* issued in 1552, which has formed the basis for all subse-quent versions, is primarily a book of services to be *read* in parish churches. How might the pattern of worship have unfolded had it been overseen by Luther? Luther, perhaps through his experience as an Augustinian monk, knew the value of music as a means to the deeper experience and under-standing of worship for all, an experience and understanding which is based not on words or rational thinking, but on a whole range of spiritual, aural, physical, emotional and psy-chological factors which we are still unable fully to explain. Cranmer and those who influenced him did not perceive the widespread value of music in worship; they perceived the elaborate music they heard as an obstacle to intelligibility and participation. It is a view which has persisted.

The repertory of English parish church music since the

Reformation has been based largely on borrowing and adding. Metrical psalms initially intended for domestic use came to be sung before and after Sunday service. In the eighteenth century hymnody was taken over from the Nonconformists. In the nineteenth century aspects of medieval and cathedral traditions were adopted for parish use. More recently there has been borrowing of responsorial usage of the post-Vatican II Roman Catholic Church, and songs, refrains and mantras from the repertories of Iona and Taizé. Metrical psalms, hymns, mission songs, choruses and worship songs often draw on popular musical idioms of their time. At the beginning of the twentieth century composers such as Vaughan Williams and Martin Shaw set out to provide durable contemporary service music apt for small parish churches. Whatever its limitations, that practice has persisted, and grown in vigour since the introduction of the Alternative Services from 1964.

Composing music for *Common Worship*

The present phase of liturgical revision, the most extensive since the Reformation, has culminated in the current cycle of publication of volumes with the collective title, *Common Worship*. In November 2000 the Church of England published two central volumes of these new liturgical orders. They contain the principal Sunday services. There is a book for the people, and a book for the President. There are also two other books published at the same time: one a volume of music for the President, the other a music resource book for the people. For the first time since the first Prayer Book of 1549 there is a concerted attempt by the Church of England to provide a substantial body of music for its liturgy.[8]

The vision has been bold, but the process has not been straightforward. There is no musical infrastructure to support the process. One looks in vain for the scholars active in research into contemporary liturgy and music to whom the

Church can turn, as they have turned to scholars of theology and liturgy. There is no musician formally attached to the Liturgical Commission. Although the Royal School of Church Music is the music agency of the Church of England its role has not been clearly defined.

Meeting with the Liturgical Commission for the first time in October 1998 it was clear that their preoccupation was, and had to be, with text. Nevertheless two important things came out of that meeting. First was the determination of the RSCM to establish a consultation to consider music for *Common Worship*. That took place in July 1999, bringing together some twenty liturgical musicians, composers and priests from a wide range of traditions and backgrounds. What was recognized was the diversity of idioms and styles we used for worship, and out of the discussions came an openness and trust which was strong and invigorating. The tangible outcome is a framework for a resource book that will draw on a range of styles of music and worship, that will include music of worth, which is accessible and technically practical, yet fresh and alive. The compilation of that book proceeds now.

The second outcome of the meeting also took place in July 1999. A task group was set up jointly by the Liturgical Commission and the Liturgical Publishing Group to address the question of music for the President's Book. That group also embarked on an agenda to reflect the range of musical styles evident in the Church, especially in the Eucharistic Prayers. Few parish churches sing any of the Eucharistic Prayer, and a tiny number sing the whole prayer. Yet the task group set out to provide two complete settings of each prayer. Why do this? Not to fulfil demand, but rather to open up possibilities. In the same way that *Common Worship* offers a resource of optional texts from which individual churches will select, so too churches can review a range of musical settings of the Eucharistic Prayers and select all or part of them.

The initial brief from the task group required one setting of each Eucharistic Prayer to be modelled on traditional Sarum chant, or a simple tone, the other to be in some way new. The challenge lay in these new settings. Prayer A was specified as 'rhythmic and upbeat', Prayer B as modern French, Prayer D as worship song, Prayer E as Taizé-like, Prayer F as Orthodox. As the only professional musician sitting round the table I found myself appointed music editor, and handling a quite remarkable brief. How does one set an extended, irregular prose text in a way that is rhythmic and upbeat? How does one catch the transient spirit of a worship song, and yet make something sufficiently durable for a book that is intended to have a life of several decades? How does one adapt the repetitive, rhyming styles of worship song lyrics to an irregular prose text? How does one make use of idioms of Taizé or the Orthodox Church without the spirituality that lies beneath them?

I felt that I could not turn to other composers without offering them some musical model that had been approved by the task group. The timetable was very tight. Everything had to be complete by the end of January 2000 to meet production deadlines. In practice the way the process has gone has been very different from what I expected. I have worked very much at the service of the task group. First drafts of six prayers went before them in September. Music and text were shuffled. Prayer D music went to Prayer E; Prayer E music to Prayer B; Prayer F needed recasting. The through-composed setting of Prayer A proved to be far too demanding; the quasi-Orthodox version of Prayer F needed to be quietly dropped. Structural issues relating to the theology of the prayers became apparent. There were also questions about the way the chant should be adapted. Which took precedence, the authenticity of the plainsong, or clear declamation of the modern texts?

In November the second submission was ready, and by now

two more prayers had been added to the quota, Prayer G and Prayer H in an early and rather lumpy draft. The new worship song settings of Prayer D (based on a pentatonic scale) and Prayer F (based on a negro spiritual) found favour. But the second version of Prayer A, in an attempt to be more periodic and straightforward, sounded like indifferent Attwood or Wesley. Prayer G with its cycle of repeated chords seemed to commend itself, as did a new version of Prayer F with a drone.

The music was also tested at a diocesan music day, and sent out to about a hundred churches for review and testing in December and January. A second consultation took place in late January, and four groups of musicians and priests worked through and revised each of the prayers. After that I retreated to Anglesey to collate the revisions of all the existing prayers, and make two settings of Prayer H, now available in a revised form.

This was an entirely new process of composition for me. First, a task group acting very much as a patron set a brief, received the work and asked for revisions, revised the brief and asked for further revisions. Second, as a result of practical testing and professional comment, the contours and details of the prayers were also subject to more change. The individuality of the composer has effectively been subjugated to the wishes of the patron, the revisions of colleagues and the scrutiny of the user. The outcome is collective rather than individual.

The materials by the beginning of February were considerable: nineteen settings of Eucharistic Prayers, provision for seasonal prefaces, additional dialogues and prayers, and alternative ways of singing the Eucharistic Prayers. On the day that the music was handed to the engraver, the committee decided that there was too much, and too much that was new and relatively untested, and that they should restrict themselves largely to Sarum chant in the President's Book. It was not a good moment; most of the work was to be abandoned. On further reflection it has become clear that there is scope for both solutions: that the traditions of the Church should be reflected in adaptations of the old chant; and that new ways of singing the whole Eucharistic Prayer should also be offered. There will therefore be a body of traditional music in the hardbound altar book, and a separate book containing a larger resource of Eucharistic Prayers, in old and new idioms.

This project shows courage and vision on the part of the Church. It is bound to be subject to criticism. It is a major step at the beginning of a slow process of formation as we review and reconsider the place and treatment of music in worship.

Composing music for worship: practical considerations

My own engagement in composing music for worship, from which this current work springs, goes back a long way. I was reminded only recently by Christopher Bishop of my first commission at the age of 11: an Anglican chant commissioned for the Wellington Festival in 1959 and broadcast on the BBC World Service! Over the years I suppose I have written per-haps five hundred pieces of music for worship, mostly small items to fulfil specific needs, the great majority unpublished. I was most active between 1972 and 1978 when I was in charge of music at St Chad's Roman Catholic Cathedral, Birmingham, and again between 1981 and 1990 at Magdalen College, Oxford. Most of the music is specifically liturgical; there are very few anthems. Some of the music is experi-mental and some intended for teaching purposes. Some little Alleluias written in 1973 for St Chad's to make them sing more rhythmically on the beat still survive in the Magdalen Eucharistic repertory; last week Magdalen were singing a Magnificat for boys' voices written partly to explore the use of *alternatim* writing and specific organ sonorities, and partly as a piece in which four or five junior boys could gain experience by singing short solos.

Compared with the amount of music I wrote for Magdalen, I commissioned very little from composers. There were two inhibiting factors. I had a concern that composers tended to think in terms of a single, self-contained work, rather than of a contributory musical object within the mosaic time-space that constitutes a form of service. Furthermore, composers do not always have a grasp of rehearsal time and the limitations of voices. And there is advantage in internal composition. Not only did the choir get used to my idioms, but I could spot ways to save rehearsal time, and as the membership of the choir changed from year to year I could allow for their strengths and weaknesses. Without realizing it I wrote very particularly for combinations of voices. Pieces written in the years when the tenor line included Paul Agnew, James Oxley, Andrew Burden and Mark Milhofer became unperformable when the character of the tenor line changed; works written for an alto line that felt tight above a' seemed far too constricted in subsequent years when William Purefoy and Robin Blaze were singing.

In shorter liturgical items I have never had any doubt about the desirability of writing singable phrases, using modal idioms, borrowing from plainsong directly or indirectly, and making harmony the servant of line. In pieces, with a capital P, I was for a long time far less comfortable. The modernist pressure to be original, to have an individual voice and to focus that individuality on a harmonic idiom seemed particularly difficult. Something of that struggle can be heard in *Lamps of Fire*, a work I wrote as an undergraduate, but which still retains its place in the Magdalen repertory.[9]

Oddly enough it was through a modernist work, Stockhausen's *Stimmung*, that I discovered a way forward, in which stasis of harmony could allow for exploration of texture, line and event. Forward-moving argument, implicit in the tensions and release of a harmonic composition, was replaced by exploration of resonance, overlaid melody and text within a shaped time frame. One of the pieces with which I am most comfortable is *Salve Regina*, written to be sung in Winchester Cathedral at the tomb of William Waynflete, founder of Magdalen, on the five hundredth anniversary of his death in 1986. It is based on the plainsong 'Salve Regina' sung daily in pre-Reformation Magdalen.

Ubi caritas is a work in a similar idiom, but more limited in its plainsong material. The text is macaronic. This setting was written to say farewell to Keith Griffin, President of Magdalen, and his wife, Dixie, in 1988. Keith Griffin was not a believer and he had concerns about the choir, indeed the college had debated the question of disbanding the choir or replacing the boys with women in the year before I was appointed. But over the years he was persuaded of the worth of the choir, supported me through some difficult patches, and even agreed to replace the organ when the college was heavily committed to other capital projects.

The work is really no more than a slow improvisation, a fantasia on the opening melody of 'Ubi caritas', and a chord of F sharp major, an exploration of melodies, resonances and textures within a time space. It was written when we had two good tenors, a good baritone and an able alto, and when we were short of rehearsal time for the boys – who therefore have an easy part. There are personal resonances in the work. *Ubi caritas* always takes me back to Mass of the Last Supper on Maundy Thursday evening at St Chad's in Birmingham, where we used to sing an English version to a melody by the Benedictine monk, Alan Rees. The boys' melody in the middle section is taken from a piece I wrote to mark the fifth anniversary of Helen House in Oxford earlier that year, another important association. The work opens by exploring the 'Ubi caritas' melody and its resonances. The middle section consists of a wash of four layers of event: a five-bar ostinato for divided tenors and basses, a statement of the chant melody in thirds and sixths for the altos, the Helen House melody for the boys, and a duet for two solo tenors – very particularly written for Mark Milhofer and Andrew Burden.

The last section returns to the opening material, varied and extended, and with a spoken text, read in the original performance by Jeffrey John, Dean of Divinity, and one of the best pastors I know. *Ubi caritas* was a piece by and for a specific group of people who worshipped daily together: they determined its nature as much as I composed it. It was an act of community.[10]

Much of my most recent work has been more down to earth, more adaptable and transferable to different circumstances. It has been concerned to explore spirituality as much as music; to see strength in melody alone as much as in textures (melody which draws on modal traditions in a straightforward, contemporary way) and to show that even where overlaid textures are used they can be sung or played by almost anyone.[11] This is music to be shared, music to be owned by those using it.

Reflecting a living tradition

Throughout this chapter I have emphasized the collective, the communal elements of writing music for liturgy. In that ambit of the collective and the communal, continuity is implicit, continuity of practice from the past, custom expressed in tradition, a word which I have deliberately avoided so far.

Our sense of tradition and of history has been distorted by artificial constructs of a past glazed in the aspic of heritage. In her recent television tour of cathedrals, Janet Street-Porter visited Winchester. There she was discomfited by the conflict between modern art and artefacts placed in a great medieval building. Many would share her view, but it is based on a series of misperceptions. The medieval builders of Winchester built in the present for the present. Those who rebuilt the choir in the fourteenth century or set up a chantry chapel in the sixteenth century built in the idiom of their day; they

juxtaposed a Norman nave, a decorated chancel and a per-
pendicular chantry. They built within a tradition that was
ongoing, alive and contemporary. They were not frightened
of bold change. When funds were available they pulled down
what was old-fashioned and replaced it.

When a cathedral choir sings a piece by Francis Grier or
Jonathan Harvey in a medieval building there is no conflict of
visual and aural styles. When they sing Gibbons or Tye or
medieval chant, they are not setting about historical recon-
struction. They are using music for worship, drawing on a
received resource and making it alive, as Christians have done
through the ages. The juxtaposition and superimposition of
historical artefacts in a living present is part of the essence of
the Christian experience. Newness, novelty is not an issue;
constant renewal lies at the heart of Christianity; it is a living
tradition. Anyone who writes for Christian worship has to be
part of that continuity.

Whenever the priest blesses the bread and the wine a past
and a present become one. The institution of the Last Supper
on Maundy Thursday is embodied in the celebration of the
Eucharist in the present. And it is not one past but many, not
one present but many; for in the thanksgiving we join with all
those who have offered bread and wine at Mass or Holy
Communion through the ages, all who offer bread and wine
today. That is a living tradition rooted in history, a collective
celebration that is at the same time individual to each of
us who seeks salvation. How then do we reflect that living
tradition in the music of the Church?

Our cultural reference points often seem shallow and disparate. We may listen to a negro spiritual in a room fashioned
in Japanese style, eating Italian food, and drinking American
cola. Equally we may dress in second-century Roman gar-
ments in a medieval Gothic building, and stand around a
nineteenth-century table singing seventeenth-century music
under twentieth-century lights. Christianity drew on its

Jewish roots and moved across the Mediterranean to Africa, to Asia, to Greece, to Rome and Western Europe. And where it moved it both adopted local culture and influenced that culture.

While we may look in vain for a new church music, I hope we would not be ashamed of something which emerges that is distinctive in style and idiom from other musics. Certainly we hope in vain for a single repertory or a single style of music for worship. But in accepting the diversity of cultural reference points open to us we can make counterpoint with the Christian past or with other Christian presents. But we have to engage with those artefacts and make them our own. Stylish singing of a medieval motet or a Russian Kontakion, an Iona song or a Latin chant will not of itself enrich the worship. External and distant objects have to become as much a part of a worshipping community as new music made in our midst.

Our challenge as clergy, musicians and composers within our respective Christian communities is to seek out the Spirit and to do our best to keep its breath alive through prayer made vibrant through music, through music made vibrant through prayer. If *we* lack the courage to explore the creative and the visionary, to take risks and make mistakes, what can we expect of the Church at large?

Notes

Chapter 1. Introduction

1 Peter Brierley, *The Tide Is Running Out: What the English Church Attendance Survey Reveals* (London, 2000); see also Callum Brown, *The Death of Christian Britain* (London and New York, 2001).

2 Sally Morgenthaler, *Worship Evangelism* (Grand Rapids, 1995), 18–22.

3 For accessible treatments of postmodernity and post-Christendom as they apply to the churches' life and mission, see Graham Cray, 'The Eucharist and the Post-Modern World', in Pete Ward (ed.), *Mass Culture: Eucharist and Mission in a Post-Modern World* (London, 1999), 74–94; Stuart Murray, *Church Planting: Laying Foundations* (Carlisle, 1998; Scottdale, PA, 2001), 175–202.

4 Ramsay MacMullen, *Christianizing the Roman Empire (AD 100–400)* (New Haven, CT, 1984), 83.

5 For a description of belief, belonging and behaviour in Christendom, see Alan Kreider, *The Change of Conversion and the Origin of Christendom* (Harrisburg, PA, 1999), 90–8.

6 Brierley, *Tide*, 9–10.

7 Brierley, *Tide*, 78.

8 *Church Times*, 17 December 1999, 1.

9 Philip Jenkins, *The Next Christendom: The Coming of Global Christianity* (New York, 2002).

10 Harvey Cox, *Fire from Heaven: The Rise of Pentecostal Spirituality and the Reshaping of Religion in the Twenty-first Century* (London, 1996), 121.

11 J.N. Hillgarth (ed.), *Christianity and Paganism, 350–750* (Philadelphia, PA, 1986), 152.

12 For discussions of inculturation, see Anscar Chupungco, *Liturgies of the Future* (New York, 1989); David J. Bosch, *Transforming Mission: Paradigm Shifts in Theology of Mission* (Maryknoll, NY, 1991), 447–57; Alan R. Tippett, Tetsunao Yamamori and Charles R. Taber, *Christopaganism or Indigenous Christianity?* (Pasadena, CA, 1975).

13 Andrew F. Walls, 'The Gospel as the Prisoner and Liberator of Culture', in his *The Missionary Movement in Christian History: Studies in the Transmission of Faith* (Maryknoll, NY, 1996), 7–9.

14 John Francis Kavenaugh, SJ, *Following Christ in a Consumer Society: The Spirituality of Cultural Resistance* (Maryknoll, NY, 1981), 16–17.

15 A helpful exercise in the many dimensions of discernment is Frank Burch Brown, *Good Taste, Bad Taste, and Christian Taste: Aesthetics in Religious Life* (New York, 2000).

Chapter 2. Music and Mystery

1 Howard Goodall, *Howard Goodall's Big Bangs* (London, 2000).

2 *Marlborough Canticles*, recorded by Christ Church Cathedral Choir, dir. Stephen Darlington (ASV CDDCA 1028).

Chapter 3. God, Theology and Music

1 This article, which first appeared in its entirety in *New Blackfriars*, 81 (January 2000), 16–26, had two sources: the first half, which was completely off the cuff; and the second half, which was based on an article in James Conroy (ed.), *Catholic Education – Inside Out, Outside In* (Dublin, 1999).

2 *Busqueda*, recorded by the Scottish Chamber Orchestra, dir. James MacMillan (Catalyst CD 09026 62669-2); *Cantos Sagrados*, recorded by Polyphony, dir. James MacMillan (Catalyst CD 09026 68125-2).

3 *The Confession of Isobel Gowdie*, recorded by the Scottish Chamber Orchestra, dir. Osmo Vänskä (BIS CD 1169).

4 James MacMillan, *Adam's Rib for Brass Quintet* (London, 1994–5);

recorded by the Scottish Chamber Orchestra, dir. Joseph Swensen (BIS CD 1019).

5 In Reginald Heber (ed.), *The Whole Works of the Right Rev. Jeremy Taylor* (London, 1822), vol. 15, 1665.

6 Gilbert Márkus, 'The Potency of God the Father', *Spirituality*, 3 (November/December 1995), 155.

7 John McDade, 'A Deathless Song', *The Month* (January 1994), 2.

8 Rowan Williams, *Open to Judgement: Sermons and Addresses* (London, 1994), 248.

Chapter 4. Darkness to Light, Cycles and Circles: The Sacred in My Music

1 *The Child of Light*, in *The Chester Book of Carols* (London, 1985), recorded by The Elysian Singers of London, dir. Matthew Greenall (Continuum CCD 1043); *At the Round Earth's Imagined Corners* (London, 1992), recorded by the Choir of St Paul's Cathedral, dir. John Scott, on vol. 3 of *The English Anthem* (Hyperion CDA 66618).

2 E.H. Gombrich, *Styles of Art and Styles of Life*, The Reynolds Lecture, Royal Academy of Arts (London, 1991), 13–15.

3 Cited in Baresh Hoffmann and Helen Dukas, *Einstein* (London, 1975), 222.

4 Sir Roger Penrose, *The Emperor's New Mind: Concerning Computers, Minds, and the Laws of Physics* (Oxford, 1989), 545.

5 Igor Stravinsky and Robert Craft, *Expositions and Developments* (London, 1962), 77.

6 'Live' interview with Halsey Stevens, in notes to *The Music of Arnold Schoenberg*, vol. 3 (CBS Records, 1965).

7 *The Ring of Eternity* and *Chamber Symphony: The Circles of Light* are recorded by the BBC Symphony Orchestra and the London Sinfonietta, dir. Oliver Knusson (EMI CDM 5665302); *In the Beginning*, performed by the BBC Symphony Orchestra, dir. Matthias Bamert (Collins CD 20032).

8 *Music to Celebrate the Resurrection of Christ*, recorded by the English Chamber Orchestra, dir. Steuart Bedford (Collins CD 20032).

Chapter 5. Requiem for Magnificat

1 *Benedicite* (Oxford, 1989).

Chapter 6. Beyond a Mass for Westminster

1 Recorded by Westminster Cathedral Choir, dir. James O'Donnell (Teldec 3984-28069-2).

Chapter 7. Worship in Spirit and in Truth

1 *Apostolic Tradition*, 21, in G.J. Cuming (ed.), *Hippolytus: A Text for Students*, 2nd ed. (Bramcote, Notts., 1987), 22.
2 Robert Webber, *Worship Old and New* (Grand Rapids, MI, 1982), 56.
3 Danyun, *Lilies Among Thorns*, transl. Brother Dennis (Tonbridge, Kent, 1991), 30–1, 70–1.
4 John Piper, *Let the Nations Be Glad! The Supremacy of God in Missions* (Leicester, 1993), 11.

Chapter 8. The Lost Tradition of Lament

1 John L. Bell, 'A Cradling Song', to tune 'Jennifer', in *When Grief Is Raw: Songs for Times of Sorrow and Bereavement* (Glasgow, 1997), 88–9.

Chapter 9. The Future of the Hymn

1 Donald Webster, *The Hymn Explosion and its Aftermath*, Address delivered at Leeds Parish Church to the Church Music Society, 1992, 16.
2 J.R. Watson, *The English Hymn* (Oxford, 1997), 532.
3 Quoted in John Julian, *A Dictionary of Hymnology* (London, 1915), 323.
4 Cited in Richard Arnold, *The English Hymn: Studies in a Genre* (New York, 1995), 1.
5 E.g., Job 38.4–7.

6 Arnold, *The English Hymn*, xiii.

7 Susan S. Tamke, *Make a Joyful Noise to the Lord: Hymns as a Reflection of Victorian Social Values* (Athens, OH, 1978), 2.

8 *Lyra Germanica*, 1ˢᵗ ser. (London, 1855), vii–viii.

9 Watson, *The English Hymn*, 493.

10 Tamke, *Make a Joyful Noise*, 9.

11 Watson, *The English Hymn*, 493.

12 London, 1967.

13 Hallam Tennyson, *Tennyson: A Memoir* (London, 1899), 754.

14 London, 1989.

15 *Songs for the New Millennium: Breaking the Chains* (Peterborough, 1999).

Chapter 10. Is there a Future for the Church Musician?

1 This is a development of ideas given earlier expression in an article in *Reformed Liturgy and Music* (the journal of the Congregational Ministries Division of the Presbyterian Church USA), 21, no. 2 (1997), 126–31.

2 John Bell, 'The Lost Tradition of Lament', in this volume.

3 In this context an interesting aside. A few years ago in a Roman Catholic journal on church music I was reading about worship in the contemporary Roman Catholic parish. The worship song 'They'll know we are Christians by our love' was mentioned and a brief, parenthetical comment was included to inform the reader that this was a 'popular' worship song from the 1960s. In the next paragraph, 'A mighty fortress' was mentioned. No parenthetical comment was provided – none was necessary.

4 Marva J. Dawn, *Reaching Out Without Dumbing Down: A Theology of Worship for the Turn-of-the-Century Culture* (Grand Rapids, MI, 1995), 93.

5 Peter Gomes, 'Religion as Spectator Sport', *The New York Times*, Thursday, 28 November 1996.

6 'The king of love my shepherd is', arr. John Ferguson, GIA Publications G-4011.

7 For recordings of my work, which contain many hymn concer-

tatos, see *Te Deum* (GIA CD 321) and *A Thousand Ages* (GIA CD 474). Both recordings, which are live and include congregational participation, model my philosophy of church music and especially my conviction that a fine choir can enable an entire congregation to find its voice.

Chapter 11. Renewing the Past in the Present: The Living Art of Church Music

1 *Common Worship: Services and Prayers for the Church of England* (London, 2000).

2 John Harper, *The Forms and Orders of Western Liturgy from the Tenth to the Eighteenth Century: Historical Introduction and Guide for Students and Musicians* (Oxford, 1992).

3 Henry and Sidney Cowell, *Charles Ives and his Music* (New York, 1955), 24.

4 Telephone conversation, 6 March 2000.

5 This is being prepared by the RSCM, in consultation with the Royal College of Organists and the Guild of Church Musicians. It will be offered by distance learning with a strong link to the national framework of higher education through a university.

6 Following the economic model set out by Charles Handy (*The Empty Raincoat* [London, 1995], 175–9).

7 After the Reformation and until 1690 the Chapel Royal, based principally at Whitehall Palace, was the outstanding choral foundation in England and Wales. It was the centre of employment and of musical creativity for church musicians, providing a model for others, especially in the seventeenth century. At present the trend is towards diversification which will prove unsustainable. Already Wells Cathedral has had to cut back on its ambitious scheme to provide for girl choristers on a par with boys.

8 *Music for Common Worship I: Music for Sunday Services*; *Music for Common Worship II: Music for the President*; *Music for Common Worship III: A Basic Guide* (all three ed. John Harper) (Westhumble, Royal School of Church Music, 2000).

9 'Love bade me welcome' and 'Set me as a seal' from *Lamps of Fire*

are recorded by the choir of Magdalen College, Oxford, dir. Grayston Ives, in *Praise to the Holiest* (Isis CD034).

10 *Salve Regina* and *Ubi caritas* are recorded by the choir of Magdalen College, Oxford, dir. John Harper, in *The English Anthem*, vol. 5 (Alpha CDCA 915).

11 As in *Come, Lord, Come* (RSCM, 1998) and *The Litany of the Thorns* (RSCM, 2000), compilations for Advent and Lent respectively, which include a substantial number of settings by David Adam. A setting of Psalm 121 from *Come, Lord, Come* has been recorded by the University of Newcastle University (NSW) Chamber Choir, dir. Philip Matthias (Chartreuse CRCD 2000).